HOW

GREAT

IDEAS

HAPPEN

The Hidden Steps Behind Breakthrough Success

George Newman

SIMON & SCHUSTER
New York   Amsterdam/Antwerp   London
Toronto   Sydney/Melbourne   New Delhi

Simon & Schuster
1230 Avenue of the Americas
New York, NY 10020

Copyright © 2026 by George Newman

All rights reserved, including the right to reproduce this book or portions thereof in any form whatsoever. For information, address Simon & Schuster Subsidiary Rights Department, 1230 Avenue of the Americas, New York, NY 10020.

First Simon & Schuster hardcover edition January 2026

SIMON & SCHUSTER and colophon are registered trademarks of Simon & Schuster, LLC

Simon & Schuster strongly believes in freedom of expression and stands against censorship in all its forms. For more information, visit BooksBelong.com.

For information about special discounts for bulk purchases, please contact Simon & Schuster Special Sales at 1-866-506-1949 or business@simonandschuster.com.

The Simon & Schuster Speakers Bureau can bring authors to your live event. For more information or to book an event, contact the Simon & Schuster Speakers Bureau at 1-866-248-3049 or visit our website at www.simonspeakers.com.

Interior design by Carly Loman

Manufactured in the United States of America

1   3   5   7   9   10   8   6   4   2

Library of Congress Control Number is available.

ISBN 978-1-6680-2600-7
ISBN 978-1-6680-2602-1 (ebook)
ISBN 978-1-6682-2744-2 (Int Exp)

Let's stay in touch! Scan here to get book recommendations, exclusive offers, and more delivered to your inbox.

For Rachel and Loa—two of the greatest explorers I know.

Contents

Introduction:
Dig for Fire

Where does creativity come from? Ask most people, and they'll tell you that great ideas come from within us—a mysterious well of human ingenuity and spirit. This view casts creativity as a sort of inner magic, a rare gift possessed by a special few. And, admittedly, that's how it can feel to have a new idea. A switch flips, a spark ignites, an epiphany happens. An idea, which didn't exist before, suddenly does.

But listen closely to history's most celebrated creators, and you'll hear something different. They describe their greatest work not as something they conjured, but as something they found. Not as invention, but as discovery. They talk of standing on the shoulders of giants, of patiently searching for just the right combination of elements, of capturing that first ember of promise and following it where it leads. Their language is that of explorers, not magicians.

This tension has fascinated me for as long as I can remember. With a pair of classical musicians for parents, a gifted pianist for a brother, and myself an aspiring visual artist, our home was often swirling with discussions of *greatness*: What made Ella Fitzgerald choose that phrasing, emphasize *that* syllable? How did Mark Rothko convey so much emotion with such simple forms? Questions like these were an endless source of curiosity and wonder.

And they still are. Even though I traded in my paintbrushes for a laptop and an academic career a while ago, I've continued to puzzle away at those same questions—not only in everyday banter with family and friends, but also in the lab, using the tools of cognitive science. I've investigated topics ranging from our appreciation of art to how we think about human potential, to the cognitive mechanics of creativity itself. Those studies have been published in leading academic journals, and their results will be woven throughout this book.

But the single most startling conclusion from my nearly two decades of research boils down to this: Those celebrated creators were right all along. Creativity is not a process of conjuring ideas out of thin air. Rather, it more closely resembles a process of *discovery*.

Consider Thomas Edison, inventor of the lightbulb, synonymous with creativity and genius. The reality? Edison didn't work alone. He led an army of nearly two hundred inventors and creatives who filled countless notebooks with failed prototypes and false starts. He preached that ideas are discovered (not created), and he regularly, and sometimes ruthlessly, borrowed from the work of others. Edison was not manifesting brilliant ideas from within—he was an explorer of possibilities, aided by hundreds of other skilled professionals at his side.

For many, creativity doesn't fit the genius myth at all. It is more like tapping into an external power grid than having a private lightbulb moment.

Which isn't to say that finding a great idea is simply luck, or that talent and expertise don't matter. They do. But the latest science reveals something surprising: Creative success depends far more on how people draw on the ideas all around them than on their innate ability. Whether we're examining creativity's inner workings in the lab or studying thousands of careers at once, we see that creative break-throughs arise from the connections we make and the opportunities we open ourselves to. They emerge from knowing when to experiment and when to drill down, and from being able to recognize when an idea holds promise in the first place.

Let's abandon the outdated notion of creative genius and replace it with something more useful: the *creative explorer*, someone who searches for new ideas with curiosity and wonder. This science-based approach reimagines creativity as an exciting journey of discovery open to everyone—not a rare gift but a universal human capacity waiting to be unlocked through exploration and connection. Instead of a lightning rod, passively waiting for inspiration to strike, imagine yourself as an adventurer, searching for your next great idea.

The Dig

In this book, I'll invite you to think about creativity like an archeol-ogist on a dig, approaching the creative process in a series of stages:

Stage 1: Surveying: Deciding where to search for ideas

Many people think of brainstorming as the first stage of creativity, but in part I, we'll see why Digging randomly rarely turns up anything of note. Instead, I'll show you how skilled creators first survey their terrain, learning to recognize promising ground and identify the right problems to solve. Drawing on both scientific research and practi-cal examples, we'll explore proven techniques for retracing the steps of others. We'll also discuss how to develop your skills as a problem finder, and why it's important to be wary of your expectations about where good ideas reside.

Stage 2: Gridding: Organizing your search

Picture the grid lines that archeologists string up over their dig sites, partitioning the field into manageable sections. In a similar manner, part II will introduce powerful tools for Gridding—ways of making your search for ideas more organized and systematic. We'll discuss the importance of forming a guiding question that serves as a compass for your search. We'll explore the benefits of thinking *inside* the box, using limitations to your advantage. And we'll unpack practical methods for how to transplant existing concepts from one domain to another to realize something entirely new.

Stage 3: Digging: Unearthing promising ideas

Next, it's time to dig. As in archeology, the goal at this stage is to get as many ideas out of the ground as possible. But in part III, we'll see why this is often easier said than done. We'll discuss fascinating research demonstrating people's tendency to stop generating ideas too early. We'll also see why it's essential to separate idea generation from idea selection. And we'll learn how to identify "sparks"—nascent ideas that are intuitively compelling, generative, and often uncomfortable.

Stage 4: Sifting: Choosing which ideas to pursue

Finally, we'll sift, learning to analyze our discoveries and select which ones to pursue further. This stage requires a very different mindset from earlier ones—careful analysis, critique, and a healthy dose of pessimism. We'll discuss the power of subtraction. We'll also consider why we shouldn't always trust our gut feelings, and how to ensure that you are learning as much as possible from your creative setbacks and triumphs.

Each chapter will bring these abstract themes to life with concrete examples from the arts, sciences, and industry. I'll explain why *Top Chef* contestants get eliminated (and where home chefs go wrong too). I'll show what distinguishes musical artists with sustained careers from those who remain one-hit wonders. I'll highlight the triumphs of Korean cinema, the genesis of Paul Simon's *Graceland*, and a cognitive error that led to a meme-worthy pet swindle. I'll show how the initial spark of an idea has an unexpectedly outsized effect on its long-term potential and why artworks produced hundreds of years apart may captivate viewers for the same underlying reasons.

This book is also packed with many practical exercises to bring these concepts to life. The exercises appear at the end of each chapter. They're designed to work either as stand-alone activities or can be combined to target a specific stage of the creative process.

I'm sure that you have your own perspective on creativity and methods that work for you. So, think of this book like a buffet: Take the concepts and strategies you find useful. Take a second helping if you like and leave behind what doesn't suit your taste. Dig in, experiment, and enjoy the process of discovery as you make this book your own.

Like an archeologist who depends on both careful attention to detail and a well-honed sense for where to look, we'll see that arriving at a great idea is not a natural gift bestowed on us at birth. Nor is it a divine visitation that allows us to magically conjure novelties out of thin air. Rather, it is about learning to explore—which means that creative breakthroughs aren't limited to a gifted few. They are available to anyone willing to learn the tools of discovery.

The truth is that we're all capable of finding a great idea within our lifetimes (or lunchtimes). The key is knowing where to look, how to dig, and how to sift and sort.

And just because there's a method to creativity doesn't mean it can't still be fun. My hope is that this book will enrich your next creative adventure—not just the final product, but the process too.

PART I

Surveying

My so-called inventions already existed in the environment—
I took them out. I've created nothing. Nobody does.
There's no such thing as an idea being brain-born;
everything comes from the outside.

—THOMAS EDISON

Kamoya Kimeu was born in rural Kenya. The son of goat herd-ers, he left school at an early age to work on the family's farm. In 1960, when Kimeu was in his late teens, he answered a job ad from the famous paleontologist couple Mary and Louis Leakey. Knowing nothing of paleontology, he later recalled, "I thought we were coming to dig some graves of dead people." Kimeu never imag-ined that he'd go on to discover more hominid fossils than any other person in history.

What distinguished Kimeu was his extraordinary ability to read the terrain, notice slight variations in the landscape, and identify promis-ing sites for excavation. Mary and Louis Leakey's son, Richard, once told an interviewer, "To some of our visitors who are inexperienced in fossil-hunting, there is something almost magical in the way Kamoya or one of his team can walk up a slope that is apparently littered with nothing more than pebbles and pick up a small fragment of black, fossilized bone."

Countless reports note Kimeu's ability to spot slight disturbances in the landscape from great distances, such as when, in 1964, Kimeu was walking up a narrow ravine when he happened to glance up and notice a tiny white object located very far up the cliff face. When he made his way to the site and brushed away the earth, an intact jawbone twinkled back at him. Or there was the time in 1975 when Kimeu and his team were hired by geologist Ron Watkins and paleontologist John Harris. "Within ten minutes of arriving," recalled Watkins, Kimeu and his Hominid Gang (as they came to be known) had already found something.

Kimeu was so expert at finding paleontological treasure that many of the researchers who traveled to Kenya in search of their next career-making discovery relied exclusively on Kimeu and his team to locate and recover new finds.

While Kimeu clearly possessed talents that made him well suited to fossil hunting—attention to detail, keen eyesight, and an analytical mind—his abilities were not innate, nor were they magic. Rather, they were the product of years of accumulated knowledge and skill.

Kimeu had spent his lifetime wandering the terrain of rural Kenya and knew its intricacies as well as anyone. He could detect the small deviations in the rock or soil that suggested the possibility of something buried below. And because he knew the terrain, he could readily integrate new information about which clues led to finds and which did not.

We know this because while Kimeu was exceptional in his ability to find fossils, he possessed something that could be taught to others. Kimeu is personally responsible for training dozens of fossil finders, and today many of Kenya's best prospectors can trace their professional lineage to him.

Discovery Takes More Than Luck

Kimeu's abilities exemplify the notion of Surveying—an ability to read the landscape, hunt for clues, and identify tiny fragments of something promising buried below. In creative endeavors, there's also a form of Surveying. But instead of searching for fragments of fossil or bone, one searches for the spark of an idea, hidden within a vast conceptual realm.

In this section, we'll learn how to effectively survey in the creative process. There is an expertise to knowing where to look for ideas and a method for finding them—one that can be taught, cultivated, and refined. We'll discuss how viewing ideas as independent from us can inform our basic tendencies to look outward (versus inward) as we embark on a creative journey, and why that's important for both our output and motivation.

We'll also explore the benefits of following in others' footsteps and how the real spark of creativity often lies in what's new to *us*, not necessarily what is new to the world. And, like the fossil hunter Kimeu, we'll come to understand the benefits of attending closely to the environment, noticing every detail in the terrain, and using that information to form hypotheses about where new and promising ideas reside.

Like unearthing a fossilized treasure, the most valuable creative insights often require both the right tools and a trained eye. So, let's begin as we develop this vital skill of Surveying—learning to spot the glimmer of possibility in unexpected places. After all, your next great discovery could be lying just beneath your feet.

1.

Burn the Cabin Down

Creativity—the generation of new and useful ideas—is at the heart of nearly everything that humans do. It provides the lens through which we examine our own existence in art, music, and literature. It is the engine that drives better and more efficient solutions in science and technology, propelling our species forward.

But at some point, the creative engine breaks down. We begin generating ideas that are not so new or not so useful. Perhaps we're unable to generate anything at all. As the journalist Gene Fowler once said, "Writing is easy; all you do is sit staring at the blank sheet of paper until the drops of blood form on your forehead."

And it's not just writers or artists who experience creative blocks. We could just as easily talk about biologists' block, entrepreneurs' block, or engineers' block.

So, what do you do when you hit a creative block? Where do you go? As I write this, my two-year-old daughter is running around the house oscillating between hysterical screaming and maniacal laughter. My ideal location in this moment? To use my daughter's words, "away."

But where do *you* go, in a perfect world? Close your eyes and imagine the place. Where is it? What does it look like? Who are you with?

If you're like many people, your mind races to the woods. And not just any location in the woods. More likely than not, it's a small cabin, secluded and quiet.

There you sit. Alone with your thoughts, waiting for that moment of brilliance. Something new. Something bold. Something unlike anything anyone has ever seen. A sudden bolt of lightning that causes you to jump up and begin furiously typing or sloshing paint on canvas. You wait for your inner creative potential—the perfect idea—to finally be unlocked.

Most of us don't have an isolated cabin in the woods, and even if we did, we probably couldn't find the uninterrupted time to use it. But the image is nonetheless powerful. Even if we can't get away in a literal sense, this view of creativity still influences our behavior.

Maybe instead of going to a cabin in the woods, you isolate yourself. Perhaps you see your friends or colleagues less. You buy noise-canceling headphones or a fancy notebook (reserved for deep thoughts only). You turn to books that say to conquer your fears, become more courageous, or engage in deep, self-reflective analysis. And maybe—if you're like many people—you start to feel that twinge of anxiety if nothing brilliant comes. You begin to question yourself as you try even harder to unlock your inner genius.

The problem with this approach to creativity is not that it is impractical or that it makes us feel bad. The problem is that this whole way of thinking is simply wrong. Those behaviors—isolating oneself, limiting outside influences, cutting off communication—do not make most of us more creative. In fact, it's the opposite behaviors, and a completely opposite way of thinking, that are more likely to succeed.

Take the myth of Henry Thoreau's Walden. Perhaps the most famous isolated cabin in the woods, Thoreau's Walden is often romanticized as the ultimate retreat for deep, solitary thought. The reality, however, is that Walden Pond was less than half a mile from Concord, Massachusetts. Thoreau threw dinner parties, and he regularly walked to town to visit with family and fellow authors like Ralph Waldo Emerson and Nathaniel Hawthorne. He even threw an annual melon party, which featured his famous homegrown watermelons. Isolated, he was not.

So, burn it down. The isolated cabin, the inner genius, the anxiety and guilt—all of it.

Forget the isolated cabin in the woods; creativity thrives on collaboration, exploration, and feedback.

The way we think about creativity has a profound effect on how we approach it in our daily lives. Consider a fascinating study that identified a key factor distinguishing creative professionals—successful musicians and actors—from the general population: their beliefs about creativity itself.

Creative professionals are more likely to view creativity as a skill that can be developed rather than an inborn marker of genius. And they reject common myths about creativity that many embrace, like that breakthroughs come from sudden inspiration or that people are their most creative when they are given no constraints.

The reason why we can be so quick to hold ourselves accountable when our creative pursuits do not live up to expectations is because we view those new ideas as coming from within. They are *our* creations, *our* inventions, entities that we manifest according to our own knowledge and will.

But what if we turn that focus inside out? What if we instead think of ideas as entities that are external to us—things that we find, respond to, and manipulate rather than conjure out of thin air? What if we approach the creative process as an opportunity for discovery, and the failure to arrive at new ideas not as a failure to generate but as an invitation to learn and explore?

Explore, Then Exploit

Throughout this book, we'll examine creativity across lots of different fields and industries—encountering many great ideas along the way. Let's begin by examining the career of Jackson Pollock, the iconic twentieth-century American painter most recognizable for his "drip" paintings.

Pollock began painting in his early twenties when he moved to New York City to live with his brother. For the next decade, he experimented with various styles ranging from abstract art to surrealism to mural painting. Eventually, his work caught the eye of the notable collector and socialite Peggy Guggenheim, and the two became friends. In 1945, Guggenheim lent Pollock the money to purchase a farmhouse in Long Island. Her hope was that a change of scenery would help Pollock recover from his struggles with alcoholism.

Shortly after his move to Long Island, Pollock began experimenting with the drip technique. His style crystallized in 1947, and by 1949, *Life* magazine catapulted Pollock to fame, asking if he was "the greatest living painter in the United States." Then, just a year later, at the peak of his notoriety, Pollock mostly abandoned his drip technique and returned to experimenting with different styles until his death in 1956.

This brief synopsis of Pollock's life may sound familiar. A talented, struggling artist unlocking his inner brilliance and forever changing art. But the tools of cognitive science have revealed surprising patterns about Pollock and his work—patterns that are true not only of Pollock but also of creatives across a wide variety of industries. These patterns challenge the conventional wisdom that great ideas come from within.

The Hot Streak. Jackson Pollock painted for two decades. But if you look closely, nearly all Pollock's iconic drip paintings were produced during a relatively brief window of time: a three-year stretch that lasted from 1947 to 1950. Once Pollock landed on the idea of the drip painting and it crystallized, that spark quickly gave rise to dozens of paintings that he produced in quick succession. A great idea took hold and propelled him forward.

What's remarkable is that this hot streak pattern isn't unique to Pollock or visual artists. In 2018, a team of researchers led by Dashun Wang at Northwestern University found that among artists, scientists, and filmmakers, hot streaks are not the exception; they are the norm. When the research team analyzed the careers of roughly thirty thousand creatives, they found that in over 90% of cases, there was evidence of a hot streak. The person arrived at a breakthrough idea and then quickly produced a flurry of related work. Winning begot winning. And this was true regardless of the domain. In other words, a great idea isn't necessarily a onetime event, but more of a pivotal concept or insight that ignites a string of connected hits.

Why does this challenge the conventional view of creativity? The popular narrative tells us that creative genius springs from natural talent and inner vision. Great ideas come from precious lightbulb moments. But what the research showed is that hitting a hot streak is not predicted by one's age, past successes, or even notoriety. Instead, it boils down to a deceptively simple three-word formula: Explore, then Exploit.

Creativity often begins in a messy, frustrating phase of searching. You experiment with false starts, chase down flimsy connections, and hit dead ends. But then, if you're lucky, something clicks. You stumble upon an idea that feels right. And that's when it's time to exploit. You shift gears from searching to executing. This is the work that turns a spark of inspiration into a blazing success.

When the Northwestern researchers looked at the data, they found that hot streaks closely followed this *exploration-to-exploitation* pattern. Artists, scientists, and filmmakers alike first went through a period of intense exploration before they zeroed in on a single idea and pushed it to its fullest potential. And the data were clear: Neither exploration nor exploitation alone could spark a hot streak. It was the sequence—the precise interplay between these two phases—that made all the difference.

This pattern tells us something profound about creative breakthroughs. When creatives hit a hot streak, it's not as if they're suddenly endowed with innate genius. Rather, they've discovered a particularly fertile idea or approach, which in turn propels a concentrated period of creative output. And these streaks do not emerge by chance, nor do they come from deep, personal reflection. They come from exploration—sifting through possibilities until something clicks that reveals not just one idea but a whole new territory to explore. Creative success isn't about waiting for genius to strike. It's about searching widely until you find an idea worth mining.

Are Some Ideas Inevitable?

Now perhaps you've looked at a Pollock drip painting and thought, *Eh, I could do that.* I mean, at first glance, Mr. Pollock's drip paintings do look a bit like someone just took a bunch of house paint and splattered it about, all willy-nilly. So, what was the *great* idea? What was the discovery? This brings us to the second fascinating pattern true of creative breakthroughs.

Multiple discovery. When physicist Richard Taylor and his colleagues used computer algorithms to analyze Pollock's drip paintings, they made a surprising discovery: The splatters and layers of paint aren't random. Instead, they conform to a complex repeating pattern, known as a fractal. In fact, it is the same fractal pattern that is observed in natural formations such as the branching of trees. This led Taylor and his colleagues to speculate that it might have been Pollock's move to Long Island—and the large trees outside his home—that inspired his shift in style.

Over time, as Pollock mined this territory, his paintings became increasingly structured. For example, in his earlier drip paintings (pre-1947), roughly 20% of the composition conformed to the fractal pattern, while in later, well-known paintings, it was as much as 90%. This suggests that Pollock wasn't simply creating random splatters but rather was discovering and refining a deep, underlying structure that resonates with human perception. Even if we don't consciously recognize the pattern, at some level our brains do, and we find it pleasurable. It mimics the same patterns we observe in nature.

What's more—and here's the part that may give you goose bumps—it's not just Pollock's paintings. A different team of scientists who were studying the Zen garden at the Ryoanji Temple in Kyoto—a World Heritage Site that has been preserved for over five hundred years—identified a similar tree-branching pattern in how the rocks in the garden were arranged. In this case, however, the pattern did not follow where the rocks were placed, but instead the negative spaces in between the rocks.

Pollock as well as the Zen monks had, in essence, made the same discovery. There was something predictable and quantifiable that made people say of a seemingly random arrangement of rocks, "That's an especially beautiful rock garden, we should preserve it for future generations." And it's the very same thing that made art collectors say of Pollock's drip paintings, "That's an especially beautiful painting; we should preserve it." In both cases, the artists, intuitively, without the use of computers or sophisticated algorithms, tapped into a deep, underlying pattern that resonates with our psychology. Fascinatingly, the pleasing effects of that resonance are evident in artworks that were produced over five hundred years apart.

This phenomenon is known as *multiple discovery*. It refers to instances when multiple independent parties discover the same idea. Just like two archeologists can discover the same excavation site, two creators can arrive at the same idea, sometimes even at the same exact time.

Multiple discovery was first documented in the academic literature over one hundred years ago, and even then, researchers noted just

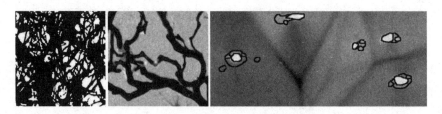

(Left panel) A fractal pattern identified in Pollock's paintings. Copyright © Richard Taylor. (Middle panel) A close-up of trees like those outside Pollock's Long Island home. Copyright © Richard Taylor. (Right panel) A truncated image of an embedded branching structure present in the Zen garden at the Ryoanji Temple. Copyright © Gert van Tonder, Michael J. Lyons, and Yoshimichi Ejma.

how prevalent it is. There aren't just one or two examples of multiple discovery in history, there are literally hundreds—and those are just the ones we know about.

Here are just a few: Charles Darwin and Alfred Russel Wallace both independently conceived of the theory of evolution by natural selection, culminating in the joint presentation of their findings in 1858; Louis du Hauron, a French physicist and inventor, and Charles Cros, a poet, independently devised the method for color photography in May 1869. Alexander Graham Bell and Elisha Gray, who were working in entirely different locations, both filed patent applications for the telephone on the same day, February 14, 1876. Wilhelm Conrad Roentgen is widely recognized for his discovery of X-rays in 1895, but Nikola Tesla had independently discovered X-rays around the same time, without being aware of Roentgen's work. The transistor was simultaneously invented in 1947 by scientists at AT&T Bell Labs as well as a team of German scientists working in Paris. Jack Kilby and Robert Noyce are both credited with independently inventing the integrated circuit in the late 1950s. The invention of the telegraph is credited to four different people, there were at least six different inventors of the thermometer, and at least nine people independently invented the telescope.

But multiple discoveries are not limited to scientific advances and technology. For example, on March 12, 1951, British comic book artist David Law and American artist Hank Ketcham both released comics about a mischievous boy titled *Dennis the Menace*. The films *Big*, *Vice Versa*, and *14 Going on 30* (all released in 1988) tell the stories of teenage boys who magically transform into adult men; *18 Again* (1988) and *Dream a Little Dream* (1989) are about elderly men in teenage bodies. Three movies released in 1994—*Terminal Velocity*, *Drop Zone*, and *Freefall*—are all action adventures built on the premise of skydiving. *Sink or Swim* (French) and *Swimming with Men* (British) are 2018 movies about middle-aged men who form synchronized swimming teams. In 2022, two documentary filmmakers—Werner Herzog (*The Fire Within*) and Sara Dosa (*Fire of Love*)—released films about the lives and work of volcanologists Katia and Maurice Krafft, who tragically died three decades earlier. The list goes on.

Professor Mark Lemley, an expert on patent law at Stanford Law School, suggests that, in fact, we should regard multiple discoveries as the norm, rather than the exception, which has important legal implications. He writes,

> *In the few circumstances where that is not true—where inventions truly are "singletons"—it is often because of an accident or error in the experiment rather than a conscious effort to invent. The result is a real problem for classic theories of patent law.*

There is a sense in which people, working completely independently from one another, may be destined to arrive at the same great idea, perhaps even at exactly the same time.

Fascinatingly, this view of inevitability in invention is thought to have been familiar to the ancient Romans and Greeks. The word invention comes from the Latin *inventio*, meaning "discovery." And according to Classics scholars, in ancient times, inventions were not viewed as independent creations, conjured from nothing. Instead, they were seen as different realizations of the same idea at different points along that idea's evolution.

Like the artistic work of Pollock and the Zen monks, these discoveries emerge across different cultures and contexts, not because of a shared history or direct influence but because they are effective responses to common needs.

Psychologist Dean Keith Simonton, who has spent his career unraveling the mysteries of how people arrive at breakthrough ideas, has drawn parallels between creativity and the process of natural selection. Just like organisms select for traits that are best suited to their environment, when people create, Simonton argues, they select for ideas that best fulfill the needs of people at that time. When multiple people feel the same creative pressures, they may be drawn to the same exact idea.

But does this mean that stumbling upon a great idea or hitting a hot streak is all a matter of chance? In short, no. As we'll see, whereas there is a significant amount of trial and error involved in the discovery of new ideas, there is also a lot that you can do to increase your chances of finding one. It's not simply "throw a bunch of spaghetti at the wall and see what sticks." Instead, there's a process—a series of steps and ways of thinking—that can dramatically improve your odds of finding something great.

Why Words Matter

In the coming chapters, we'll dive into the method of discovery itself— the nuts and bolts. But to describe why I think this view of creativity is so important, I'll share a personal anecdote. Early on in my academic career, I was given a peculiar piece of advice. One day, a senior colleague pulled me aside and said, "Succeeding here is straightforward. Just do something that changes the field."

Admittedly, I was a bit rattled. To me, this implied that coming up with a breakthrough idea was simply a matter of motivation and focus. That if I wasn't changing the field, it was either because I wasn't working hard enough, I was spending my time on the wrong things, or maybe I just didn't have it.

And I think the unfortunate reality is that this type of message is quite common—especially to young people. The message is that great ideas come from geniuses who work hard. If you haven't achieved something great, it either means you're not working hard enough or you're not a genius.

I believe, however, that this message communicates all the wrong things:

It's easy to discount the chance involved in creative discoveries.

Telling someone to buckle down and come up with something great is a bit like being plopped into rural Kenya and being told to find an important fossil that "changes everything." Not only is it impossible to simply decide to start producing great things, in many instances, it is extremely difficult to anticipate which ideas will be impactful even after we discover them. Instead, we need to emphasize the process of exploration itself. We should encourage the act of discovery, not merely the outcomes.

This first means putting in the right kind of preparation—the groundwork—which is exactly what this book is about. Just as an archaeologist can't guarantee a major fossil find, you can't guarantee a game-changing idea. However, you can significantly improve your chances, both in spotting promising ideas and recognizing their potential once found.

The superstars in your field are subject to the same principles of discovery as everyone else (as the hot streaks research reveals), but what they have mastered is a keen sense for how to search for and identify promising ideas. I believe this is what we are really referring to when we compliment someone's "taste" or "intuition." These are skills, not inborn markers of genius.

The second thing this means is that *everyone* has a shot of finding something. But in order to make creative breakthroughs truly accessible, there have to be the resources available for people to do the kind of deep work that is needed.

It's no coincidence that many celebrated creators throughout history have tended to come from economically privileged backgrounds. The real advantage these individuals have, in terms of creativity? Time. If creativity is partly a numbers game, then the more time you have, the more chances you have to hit something. From a societal perspective, this means we should aim to do everything we can to provide people—especially young people—with the time that is needed to engage in exploration as they come to know and refine their process.

Telling people to be creative freaks them out.

A second reason the "do something great" message does more harm than good is that it can induce anxiety that actually limits one's creative potential. In a clever series of experiments, Melanie Brucks and Szu-chi Huang, two psychologists at Stanford University, investigated how soliciting creative ideas ironically stifles creative output. The researchers incentivized participants to brainstorm new ideas for a variety of products, like toys, office supplies, toiletries, and mobile apps. In each case, one group of participants was asked to generate "as many creative ideas as possible," while the other group was asked to generate "as many ideas as possible" (the word *creative* was omitted).

The researchers then compared the number of ideas that participants came up with across the two conditions. Reliably they found that directives to come up with creative ideas caused people to self-impose a high standard, which restrained their thinking. This amounted to roughly a 20% decrease in productivity, leading to worse ideas in the creative condition. In later chapters, we'll see how imposing limits at the brainstorming stage can undermine the discovery of better ideas. The work of Brucks and Huang reminds us how even subtle pressures to "be creative" can ironically derail one's creativity.

If people don't succeed, they blame themselves and retreat.

Finally, if we don't come up with anything particularly great, we are all too quick to turn inward. We begin to blame ourselves. Maybe you try to find an even quieter space in an even more isolated area. You stare at the blank page, or screen, or canvas, *even harder.* The logic is always the same: Because the ideas come from within, we must concentrate and look deeper inside us.

But the notion of creative discovery points us in exactly the opposite direction. If you're feeling stuck, forget about yourself and your own pursuits for a moment and dive into someone else's work. Begin researching adjacent areas. Strike up conversations with colleagues and friends. Visit a museum or someplace totally new.

No archeologist would be excited to search a barren landscape. Similarly, you won't be excited to begin digging for ideas if there's nothing for you to learn from or react against.

Harvard professor Teresa Amabile—a giant in the study of creativity—has long advocated for the importance of situational and environmental factors in shaping creative success. Indeed, several experiments show how even small changes in your environment can have a dramatic boost on your creativity. For example, exposure to new images, people from different cultures, or even taking a walk outside can lead us to think in new, breakthrough ways. Moreover, neuroimaging studies have found that the brain structures involved in memory are activated when we integrate new ideas into creative tasks, suggesting that part of the boost we get from exposure to new ideas may come from jogging our own memories and making connections that we may not have considered otherwise.

A wonderful example of this approach comes from acclaimed author Margaret Atwood, who has won the esteemed Booker Prize twice. In her creative process, Atwood draws extensively on archives, historical records, and academic papers to inspire her stories. In *Alias Grace*, Atwood reimagines the true story of a convicted nineteenth-century murderess, incorporating many real-life events. And in writing the classic *The Handmaid's Tale*, Atwood drew extensively on real newspaper clippings unearthed from the library archives at the University of Toronto. By blending these external sources with her own process, Atwood realizes compelling narratives that get us to think about our world in bold, new ways.

Another example comes from the legendary music producer Rick Rubin, who has helped guide career-making albums for dozens of artists across a variety of musical genres—Jay-Z, Johnny Cash, Metallica, Adele, and others. Rubin is famous for inspiring the artists he works with to let go of their preconceived notions, experiment, and use what is in their immediate environment to inform their creative process. In one interview, Rubin recalled a moment when Serj Tankian, vocalist for the genre-bending band System of a Down, hit a creative block. Rubin encouraged Serj to go to his library, pick a book off the wall, turn to any page, and simply read the first line he saw. "That's what's in the song," Rubin recalled. "And it's a high point in the song; it's incredible; it's like magic."

When in Doubt, Look Out

While writing this book, there were several times when I struggled to make progress, and inevitably, the knee-jerk reaction to withdraw and retreat returned. But then, after bleeding from the forehead for a bit, I would simply begin reading, and looking, and listening. In surprisingly short order, I was inspired again, chasing down fascinating threads, filling scraps of paper with notes, on the hunt for new terrain to unearth and excavate.

Too often, the pressure to create leads us to strive for something the world has never seen. But it is important to remember that the spark of creativity often starts with what's new and exciting to *you*, not necessarily what's new to everyone.

Exercises

Surveying is all about figuring out where you will begin your search for ideas. One of the first steps in that process is identifying your own interests and motivations. To put it bluntly, if you don't care deeply about what you are working on, no one else will. Creative exploration is fueled by your own curiosity and passion. These first exercises are intended to spur your thinking about the topics and questions that you find personally meaningful.

Exercise 1: Identifying Your Passions

The goal of this exercise is to identify creative direction by reflecting on past experiences, current interests, and common threads across time.

Reflect on past experiences and make a list of the following:
- Activities, projects, or interests that you enjoyed as a child—those you excitedly looked forward to and/or had to be "dragged away" from.
- Personal achievements from the past that you feel most proud of.
- Activities you enjoyed doing but weren't necessarily immediately good at—skills that you were passionate about but had to really work to develop.

Think about your current interests and make a list of the following:

- What you currently look forward to working on. If you had an extra day of the week—responsibility free—to spend working on any creative endeavor of your choosing, what would it be?
- Anything that gives you energy, that lights you up—could be a physical activity, visiting with certain people, engaging in a particular task or hobby.
- Topics or interests that you frequently discuss with others because you find them so fascinating and fun to discuss.
- Topics that others come to you for advice about.
- Any topics, or problems, or social issues that you frequently "rant" about.
- Topics or areas of life where you feel like a true expert, with an important and original perspective to share with the world.

Look for patterns.
- Review your lists and highlight recurring themes. What common threads do you notice? What topics or interests appear again and again?
- It can also be helpful to consider projects that you have abandoned. What about these projects made you drop them? How do they compare to the other interests on your list?

What's missing?
- Are there any consistent themes, or activities, or interests you identified that you are not currently working on?
- Imagine you could hit a Pause button on the world and start any new creative project with unlimited time and focus—what would it be?
- What is the smallest possible version of this project you could start today?

Exercise 2: A Conversation About Your Passions

Conversations with others can provide a valuable window into our underlying interests and motivations. This exercise is designed to help you uncover what excites and drives you creatively. Inspired by psychologist Arthur Aron's famous set of questions that build connection through increasing self-disclosure, these prompts guide you through a similar exercise—only this time, the focus is on your creative passions.

With a trusted partner, take turns asking each other the questions below. There's no need to rush—take your time, reflect, and enjoy the back-and-forth. Some questions are light and fun, while others dig a little deeper, so go with whatever feels natural. You might just surprise yourself with what you discover!

1. If you could collaborate on a creative project with anyone, living or dead, who would it be?
2. What kind of creative work or activity makes you lose track of time?
3. Describe your perfect creative day: Where are you, what are you working on, and who are you with (if anyone)?
4. If you could instantly master one new creative skill, what would it be and why?
5. How do you hope your work impacts others? In what ways would you like your work to help people?
6. Describe the last time you felt truly excited about working on a creative idea.
7. What's a creative project you've always wanted to start but haven't? What's holding you back?
8. What's a creative idea of yours that seemed too wild or ambitious to pursue? Do you still think about it?

9. If you could join any creative community or movement from history, which one would you choose? Why?

10. If you could put a single creative work of yours in a time capsule for future generations, what would it be and why?

11. What's the best compliment you've ever received about something you created? Why did that compliment stick with you?

12. If you knew you had only a year left to live, what creative work would you most want to complete?

13. What emotion do you most often associate with your creative work? Excitement, frustration, joy, something else?

14. If you could receive an anonymous letter of encouragement from someone, what would you want it to say?

15. What's the most personal thing you've ever put into your creative work?

16. What's the biggest creative dream or ambition you've had but never shared with anyone?

Exercise 3: Finding Inspiration Through Attachments

This exercise is designed to help identify compelling topics based on things you have a strong emotional attachment to. You can use lists, or, personally, I like to use simple presentation software, like .ppt, to be able to look at images and text together.

Gather inspiration.
- **Media:** Make a list of your favorite books, films, albums, art: any media that you frequently revisit because it feels like you.
- **Places:** Make a list of the places or settings that inspire you: places you visited, places you go regularly, places where you feel most yourself.

- **Objects:** Make a list of any sentimental objects you keep: What are those objects? Why are they important to you? Jot down feelings that are associated with those objects.

Tell a story.
- Now imagine that you had to tell the "story of you" by choosing one piece of media, one place, and one object. Which three would you select?

Connect it to a project or topic.
- Is there common theme, feeling, or mood across the items you selected? Can you connect that theme to a creative project or topic that you could work on? If so, what would it look like?

Exercise 4: Your Anti-Passions

In some cases, we have a clearer sense of the things we don't want to work on than the things we do want to work on. This exercise is intended to help you identify potential creative avenues by first identifying what you *don't* want to work on.

- **Make a list of creative projects that you don't want to work on.** What do you find unappealing or boring about these topics? Next to each topic that you listed, identify what it is about those topics or types of projects you find aversive (e.g., too technical, too abstract, too predictable, too radical). For example, if you're a musician you might think, *I would never want to be in a cover band.* Well, why?

- **Try to brainstorm things that are the opposite of what you don't like.** If not *that*, what is the kind of thing you would be excited to work on?

Exercise 5: Your Perspective on Creativity

This is a short scale I developed to provide a check-in about how you generally think about creativity. For each statement, write "2" if you strongly agree, "1" if you slightly agree, "0" if you neither agree nor disagree; "–1" if you slightly disagree, and "–2" if you strongly disagree. Then sum up the numbers to see your score.

Creativity is a process of discovery,
not inventing things out of thin air.   ____

Creative breakthroughs come from building on the
ideas of others rather than from a single person's genius.   ____

The best creative ideas are sparked through collaboration.   ____

Most great ideas emerge gradually,
not in flashes of inspiration.   ____

The best ideas come from interacting
with the world around you.   ____

Great ideas are more likely to come from trial and error,
rather than a sudden moment of insight.   ____

True creativity lies in reimagining and repurposing
existing ideas,not inventing things from scratch   ____

Total: ____

Scores of 8 or above: You currently have a high explorer view of creativity.
Scores of 0 to 7: You currently have a medium explorer view of creativity.
Scores below 0: You currently have a low explorer view of creativity.

2.

Originality Ostriches

There is something to be said about a truly disastrous meal, a meal forever indelible in your memory because it's so uniquely bad, it can only be deemed an achievement. The sort of meal where everyone involved was definitely trying to do something; it's just not entirely clear what . . . I'm talking about the long tail stuff—the sort of meals that make you feel as though the fabric of reality is unraveling. The ones that cause you to reassess the fundamentals of capitalism, and whether or not you're living in a simulation in which someone failed to properly program this particular restaurant.

This excerpt is from a 2021 review of a Michelin-starred restaurant named Bros. Geraldine DeRuiter, a popular food blogger, goes on to describe course after course (twenty-seven of them in all) of what sound more like exhibits at a haunted house than elevated fine dining. Highlights include "an oyster loaf that tasted like Newark airport," a squirt of gelee infused with droplets of meat molecules, a tasting of twelve different kinds of foam, "frozen air" (whatever that is), and several pieces of flavored paper. The final dessert course was a dollop of foam served in a plaster cast of the chef's mouth. Diners were instructed to lick the foam out of the plaster mouth resulting in a scene the blogger described as "something stolen from an eastern European horror film."

The Bros. example illustrates a fundamental challenge in creative work: creating something new that people actually want. Creative ideas must offer something that is new. But equally as important, they need to provide some sort of value to people. And by value I don't mean money. Instead, I mean the concept of utility—the reason why people are drawn to a creative work in the first place, either because it nourishes them, entertains them, expands knowledge, stirs emotions, brings people together, or fulfills more practical needs.

In one episode of *The Simpsons*, Homer invents an Everything's Okay Alarm. The idea is novel, but it solves a problem that no one has. Similarly, the core problem at Bros. restaurant seems to be that in striving to be original and unlike any other dining experience, the chef forgot the most important ingredient—making the food actually taste good. Novelty came at the expense of value.

In a series of studies that I conducted with my graduate student Jin Kim, we were interested in how people balance novelty and value as they search for creative ideas. We asked people to generate ideas in a domain where most people regard themselves as expert: making sandwiches.

The participants—we referred to them as "chefs"—were asked to come up with a novel sandwich recipe. Sometimes we gave them specific prompts, but in all versions of the experiment, we asked the chefs how much they prioritized originality in their recipes and how much they focused on making their sandwiches tasty. To ensure that everyone made their sandwiches as appealing as possible, we offered cash prizes for the most-liked recipes. Interestingly, we found that our chefs thought that originality would only help. The more novel the recipe, they thought, the more attractive it would be to others.

But when we recruited a new group of participants—the "customers"—who rated the sandwich recipes in terms of how likely they would be to try them, we found exactly the opposite: Customers were significantly less likely to purchase sandwiches from chefs who had focused on being original. In fact, the more original the chefs tried to be, the less willing customers were to try their sandwiches. Given that our chefs seemed to be somewhat blind to how focusing on originality had decreased the appeal of their creations, we dubbed this phenomenon the Originality Ostrich effect.

Was this just a problem for amateur sandwich makers? We also decided to test for the Originality Ostrich effect among more experienced chefs. With the help of a team of research assistants, we coded data from multiple seasons of the popular show *Top Chef*. For each episode of the show, our research assistants took note of how the contestants talked about their dish. Did the chef say they went with an established recipe, or did they try something new? Did they mention creativity, or say they tried to be original in some way?

Interestingly, we found that much like our home chefs, focusing on originality dramatically *increased* contestants' chances of being eliminated from the competition. In fact, when *Top Chef* contestants explicitly said they focused on making something original and different from anyone else, they were more than twice as likely to have the worst-rated dish and be kicked off the show.

In this chapter, we'll discuss why the Originality Ostrich effect has important implications for Surveying and where we begin our search for successful ideas. The key insight is that when most people set out to do something "creative," their minds race to what's never been done before. But rather than looking to what has never been done, you may be far more likely to find success by considering where successful ideas have been found in the past.

As in archeology, finds tend to cluster together. So paying attention to where successful ideas have come from can provide valuable information about where other promising ideas are likely to be discovered. Past success can be one of the strongest signals that a particular creative direction is worth pursuing.

The 5% Novelty Rule

We often imagine creative breakthroughs as a radical departure from existing work. But when complex systems researcher Brian Uzzi conducted a landmark study of scientific breakthroughs, he discovered something striking: The most innovative work is built on a foundation that is exceptionally . . . conventional.

Uzzi and his colleagues undertook an extraordinary analysis of 18 million scientific articles. Using computer algorithms, the team analyzed this enormous mountain of data to understand the relationship between novelty and scientific impact. Each paper's references served as a measure of its novelty. Papers that relied heavily on research from the same field scored as highly conventional, while papers that spanned wildly different fields scored as more novel.

The upshot? The most influential research papers were not the most novel. In fact, the biggest "hits" all clustered in a particular sweet spot: research that was roughly 90% to 95% conventional and only 5% to 10% novel.

At first glance, this might seem disappointing. Does this mean we should aim to be conventional, boring even? Not at all. The surprising insight of this research was that major breakthroughs don't come from abandoning convention entirely, nor do they come from rigidly sticking to what's known. Instead, they emerge when we start with a proven idea and then carefully rework it to uncover a spark of something new.

The highest-impact science, it turns out, leans heavily on what's familiar and known while introducing just enough novelty to push the boundaries—more like remixing an existing song than composing from scratch.

In fact, remixing is exactly how fashion designer Virgil Abloh—former artistic director of Louis Vuitton and founder of the brand Off-White—described his creative process. Abloh, who revolutionized fashion by blending streetwear with luxury, famously advocated for what he called the "3% percent approach": taking an existing celebrated design and changing it by just 3%. Drawing inspiration from contemporary artists like Duchamp and Warhol, Abloh referred to this method as his "cheat code." "It's like hip-hop. It's sampling," Abloh explained. "I take James Brown, I chop it up, I make a new song."

A similar idea also appears in Bob Dylan's approach to songwriting. Raphael Falco, a professor of English at the University of Maryland, likens Dylan's creativity to that of Renaissance poets. Falco describes how hundreds of years ago, "originality" did not mean creating something out of nothing. Rather, it meant returning to what had come before: "Writers first searched outside themselves to find models to imitate, and then they transformed what they imitated into something new. . . . Just as a bee samples and digests the nectar from a whole field of flowers to produce a new kind of honey—which is part flower and part bee—a poet produces a poem by sampling and digesting the best authors of the past."

According to Falco, Dylan did something similar to these Renaissance poets with his songwriting. For example, in writing the classic song "A Hard Rain's A-Gonna Fall," Dylan repurposed the Old English ballad "Lord Randal." Falco writes: "With his own idiosyncratic method of composing songs and his creative reinvention of the Renaissance practice of *imitatio*, [Dylan] has written and performed over six hundred songs, many of which are the most significant and most significantly original songs of his time."

The world of business also has a related trend, known as the *second-mover advantage*. In many cases, it's not the original version of an idea that takes off. Rather, breakthrough business ideas often come from a slight tweak to an existing idea, such as a small change in product design, application, or even just the name. Before there was Airbnb (2008), there was CouchSurfing (2004). Before Spotify (2006), there were Rhapsody (2001) and Last.fm (2002). And when Noah McVicker invented a putty for cleaning wallpaper, it was his relative, Kay Zufall, who had the insight to reimagine it as a children's toy—Play-Doh.

Whether you're an aspiring chef, scientist, designer, musician, or entrepreneur, the recipe for success seems to be the same:

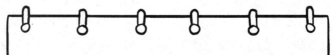

RECIPE FOR A BREAKTHROUGH IDEA

**Make the main dish conventional,
something familiar and known.**

**Then add something special—a spice or twist—
making it new, exciting, and your own.**

Does adopting the 5% novelty rule mean that we are destined to be nothing more than sprinkles or a side garnish?

Here it is essential to distinguish between the creative process versus the outcome. Think of the natural world. The slow and steady process of erosion produced the magnificent rock formations of Arches National Park. The tiny, incremental changes of evolution have produced an astounding array of biodiversity. The impacts of Abloh's designs or Dylan's songwriting have been transformational and epic. But the process that led to those creative upheavals was much more incremental—a slow, plodding crawl out of the known, one small step at a time.

Your next project doesn't need to reinvent the wheel. It just needs to make it spin a little differently. Take what inspires you and make it just a little bit better, a little bit different, a little bit more you. And in that space between what exists already and your own unique take—that vital 5%—you might find something extraordinary. After all, many of history's great masterpieces started with a simple thought: *What if I just changed this?*

Start by Emulating Your Heroes

Think about the signature style of your favorite visual artist. Perhaps it's the bold, expressive style of Vincent van Gogh, the flowing, floral motifs of Georgia O'Keeffe, or the frenetic gestures of "Cy" Twombly. Artists strive to devise their own visual language—a coherent set of materials, color palette, and subject matter; a self-contained universe of sensory information that is instantly recognizable and attributable to them. The same is true in music. We can often recognize a musical artist in seconds, simply based on their "signature sound."

But when you examine the careers of those artists and how their work developed and changed over time, few of them arrived fully formed. Instead, their journeys often began in very familiar territory, by imitating great artists who had come before. A slight move in this direction, another move in that direction, and then, bam! The artist hits upon something that takes hold, and they begin to excavate.

To illustrate this point, consider the work of Piet Mondrian, regarded as one of the pioneers of abstract art. The figure below shows how Mondrian's paintings changed over the forty years following his graduation from art school.

Examples of Piet Mondrian's work from 1900 to 1940.
Copyright ©2025 Mondrian/Holtzman Trust.

Right away, you'll notice two very different halves of Mondrian's career: exploration and then exploitation. During the first half, Mondrian experimented. You can see his style fluctuating every couple of years, as he plays with different subject matter, color palettes, and styles of painting.

He begins by emulating Dutch masters, creating representational paintings of landscapes. Then he is influenced by Post-Impressionism and begins to imitate the work of artists like Georges Seurat and Paul Cézanne. His work then gets more abstract, with the emergence of treelike formations, geometric grids, and so on. Elements of the previous style ooze into the next one.

But around 1920, there is a dramatic shift. The elements that Mondrian has been developing converge. Suddenly, he produces a flood of work that all looks very similar: a two-dimensional grid, composed of rectangles with black lines and primary colors. Mondrian had found his own signature style, and he begins to exploit it. His hot streak began.

From this point forward, Mondrian iterates endlessly on this same motif. During the second half of his career, his paintings have an almost obsessive quality as he narrows in and refines. It's as if he is trying to understand the very limits of what this combination of elements can produce and unearth all that he can from them.

What was so compelling about these grids? Why did Mondrian focus on the same design for the rest of his career instead of continuing to experiment as he had done in the past?

That's easy (you may be thinking), money and fame. But that wasn't it. For one, the notion of an "art star" didn't exist yet. Artworks didn't sell for millions. But even by the standards of his day, Mondrian was not particularly celebrated during his lifetime. For example, Mondrian didn't have his first US solo exhibition until 1942, when he was nearly seventy years old. So, if it wasn't money or fame, what was it?

Years later, computer scientists analyzed Mondrian's compositions and found that, like Jackson Pollock's drip paintings, there is a quantifiable structure that differentiates true Mondrian grid paintings from replicas that have similar appearances. Mondrian not only used branching structures and a certain density of lines; he also adhered to a precise balancing of visual weight. In his grid paintings, smaller patches of dark colors (blue and black) are offset by larger patches of light colors (red and yellow) to a startling degree of mathematical precision.

Mondrian's early years of imitation and experimentation led him to discover fundamental truths about visual balance and harmony. When he finally hit upon his signature grid style, he wasn't chasing past success. He was excavating a deep mathematical principle reflecting how our brains process visual information.

This suggests an inspiring possibility for your own creative journey. When you find that sweet spot—an idea or approach that keeps pulling you back—you might be uncovering something real and universal, hidden just beneath the surface.

Start by identifying someone whose work speaks to you, especially the people who make you think, *I wish I had done that!* Then begin to retrace their path. Don't worry about being derivative. Remember, you're not copying to produce something identical but to use as a springboard for finding your own way. Pay attention to what feels natural as well as what doesn't. These points of friction often signal where your own unique perspective is beginning to emerge.

Imitation Is About Understanding, Not Copying

Anna was not like a fashionable lady, nor the mother of a boy of eight years old. In the elasticity of her movements, the freshness and the unflagging eagerness which persisted in her face, and broke out in her smile and her glance, she would rather have passed for a girl of twenty, had it not been for a serious and at times mournful look in her eyes, which struck and attracted Kitty.

Getting lost in Leo Tolstoy's words and cadence helps you start to understand the world he's imagining in *Anna Karenina*. Now feel the difference when you let Toni Morrison's words transport you in *Beloved*:

> *She is a friend of my mind. She gather me, man. The pieces I am, she gather them and give them back to me and all the right order. It's good, you know, when you've got a woman who is a friend of your mind.*

Neither of these may be your preferred writing style, but by inhabiting these authors' words, their rhythm, their worlds, you not only emulate masters of the craft but also expand and develop your own voice. When you immerse yourself in great writing, you're not trying to become Tolstoy or Morrison. You're developing an ear for how language can move and breathe.

It's like learning a new instrument. You begin by playing others' songs, not to perform them forever, but to understand how music works. This takes the pressure off because you're not expected to create something entirely new. Instead, you're giving yourself time to absorb, understand, and eventually transform those influences into something that feels true to you. The goal is to comprehend—to grasp how these masters achieve their effects—so you can begin to discover your own path.

Artist Austin Kleon captures this beautifully in his book *Steal Like an Artist*, where he highlights the virtues of imitation. "Free from the burden of trying to be completely original," he reminds us, we can "embrace influence instead of running away from it."

But more than motivation, Kleon describes imitation as a critical learning tool—a way to reverse engineer the creations of our heroes, "much like a mechanic taking apart a car to see how it works."

Kleon is correct that imitation has deep roots in how we learn. Developmental psychologist Lev Vygotsky showed that imitation is fundamental to how we come to understand the world around us. But human imitation isn't mechanical or thoughtless. More than just imitators, we are sense makers. We don't merely copy others. We need to understand *why*.

Consider an ingenious set of experiments conducted by a team of cognitive scientists at Yale University, spearheaded by Derek Lyons and my PhD mentor, Frank Keil. The researchers presented toddlers with elaborate puzzle contraptions that contained prizes. When shown how to open the puzzles, children copied all the steps, even unnecessary ones. But they weren't copying blindly. When given a choice between a cumbersome way to perform an action and a more direct one, they consistently chose efficiency. They weren't just mimicking movements. They were trying to understand the underlying purpose.

When we imitate other people's creative work, we are forming a theory about their process—why they made certain decisions and how their creative choices relate to one another. Take Mondrian's grid paintings, for example. If you tried to create one yourself, you might start by drawing some black lines and filling in squares with primary colors. But then, you'd begin to notice subtle decisions he made. How thick should the lines be? How many squares? Why do some colored sections feel more balanced than others? Through this process of careful imitation, you would gain insights into the underlying principles that guided his work.

This act of deeply studying others, trying to re-create their work, is what I call *high-resolution Surveying*. Low-resolution Surveying involves gathering surface-level information about a wide variety of topics—knowing a little about a lot of stuff. This can be useful too, as we'll see in the next chapter. But high-resolution Surveying—

gathering exhaustive and detailed information about a very narrow topic—is the key to unlocking the learning potential of imitation. For example, you might focus on the work of a single person or even a specific portion of a person's career.

Many creative endeavors are essentially problem-solving exercises, where each step reveals new possibilities and challenges. And our unconscious mind often understands these patterns before we can articulate them. Like an iceberg, much of our creative processing happens beneath the surface. But by walking around in the mind of someone else and shadowing their creative steps, you're developing the necessary tools that will eventually guide you to your own discoveries.

Korean cinema offers a fascinating example of this approach in action. From the 1960s through the late 1980s, the Motion Picture Law severely restricted what South Korean filmmakers could produce, while simultaneously limiting the import of foreign films. This created an unusual dynamic. Aspiring filmmakers found themselves studying a limited selection of foreign films with intense focus and dedication.

This period of intense study laid the groundwork for what would later become known as the Korean New Wave. When censorship finally began to ease in the 1990s, Korean filmmakers emerged with a profound understanding of cinematic storytelling. They began creating what became known as "well-made" films—a term that reflected both their technical polish and their clever adaptation of proven narrative structures.

These films often took familiar genres or plot structures but then told those stories through a distinctly Korean lens. Park Chan-wook's *Oldboy* (2003), for instance, worked within the revenge thriller genre but infused it with uniquely Korean themes about shame and family honor. Bong Joon-ho's *Memories of Murder* (2003) used the serial killer genre to explore the country's transition from military dictatorship to democracy. Kim Jee-woon's *A Bittersweet Life* (2005) drew on the cool aesthetics of Jean-Pierre Melville's gangster films while examining specifically Korean concepts of loyalty and social hierarchy.

The success of Korean cinema demonstrates how mastery through imitation can lead to genuine innovation. Through careful study of foreign films, Korean filmmakers developed the tools to express their own unique voices and cultural perspectives. The result was the emergence of a distinctive national cinema that speaks both to universal human experiences and to specifically Korean concerns.

Effective Surveying—knowing where to look for successful ideas—requires balancing convention with novelty. And people often get this balance wrong. They focus too much on the novelty piece, creating dishes no one wants to eat or avant-garde films that most audiences can't (and don't want to) follow. But as we've seen from Mondrian's grids to Korean cinema, creative breakthroughs often come from deeply understanding and imitating what has worked before.

The beauty of this approach lies in what Austin Kleon calls "our wonderful flaw." Human beings are incapable of making perfect copies. Our failed attempts to imitate our heroes inevitably reveal our own unique perspective. In those small imperfections and adaptations, we discover our voice. As Kleon puts it, "Our failure to copy our heroes is where we discover where our own thing lives. That is how we evolve."

Exercises

Throughout this chapter, we've seen how creative breakthroughs often emerge not from radical reinvention but from carefully studying and building upon what's worked before. These exercises are designed to get you thinking about the interplay between novelty versus convention and where others have found creative success.

Exercise 6: Unlocking New Ideas

Explore how adding small elements to an existing shape can open new possibilities. This exercise will help you think about how minor changes can lead to innovative breakthroughs for lots of different types of projects.

- **Select a shape.** From the set of shapes below, select one that resonates with you. It could be a shape that feels incomplete or one that sparks curiosity.

- **Make a change.** Without overthinking, add a detail to the shape. It could be an extension, an outline, or something that interacts with the original form (a line through the shape, an internal cutout, an extra stroke along the edge). Does this change unlock any new ideas for what it could represent or become?

- **Make another change.** Build on the first addition by introducing a second small change. This could be a different texture, another line, or a subtle transformation in one section. Ask yourself again, how has this new change altered the shape? Does it evoke a new purpose? Do new associations or ideas come to mind?

- **Iterate with a third change.** Make a third modification. This should be another minor but meaningful change. Could a small piece of the shape be repeated, echoed, or mirrored? What possibilities are emerging as a result of these combined tweaks?

- **Evaluate.** Review the modified shape. What has the process of adding small elements revealed? Could this approach be applied to other areas of your work or thinking? Reflect on the idea that small, deliberate changes can unlock larger, unexpected breakthroughs. Select another shape from the set and repeat the process.

Exercise 7: The 5% Workshop

This exercise helps you practice finding the sweet spot between convention and novelty by deliberately constraining your creative changes to just 5% of an existing work.

- **Select a piece of creative work you admire** (something relatively simple that you could actually emulate)—e.g., a short story, a poem, a song, a drawing.

- **Copy the work.** To the best of your ability recreate the work identically, word for word, line for line, or note for note.

- **Brainstorm** at least ten different ways you could modify just 5% while keeping the rest intact.

- **Pick your favorite change** and actually try it out. Then, experiment with a different change, and another after that. Notice how these subtle changes begin to alter the nature of the work.

Exercise 8. Interview Your Hero

The goal of this exercise is to develop a richer understanding of your hero's motivations and decision-making by conducting an imagined interview with them.

- **Choose a creative hero**—living or deceased—whose work you admire and wish to emulate.

- **Prepare a list of interview questions** that cover a wide range of topics, including career choices, challenges, motivations, and views on creativity. Here are some sample questions to get you thinking:
    1. What life experiences most influenced the way you think about your work?
    2. What is the most important idea you ever had, and why does it matter?
    3. If someone wanted to follow in your footsteps, what should they focus on mastering?
    4. What habits or routines helped you stay productive?
    5. How did collaboration or rivalry shape your ideas?
    6. How did you decide when an idea was truly great and worth pursuing?

7. What inspired you most throughout your career?
8. How did you handle failure or ideas that didn't work out?
9. What do people often misunderstand about your work?

- **Research your creative hero** to gather as much information as possible about their thoughts through interviews and/or biographies. If you know your creative hero and can actually talk with them, even better!

- **Use the information you've gathered** to answer each interview question from the perspective of your hero. If there are gaps in the information, use your understanding of their character and philosophy to help fill in the blanks.

- **Document your mock interview** in a concrete format, such as a written transcript, that you can revisit later.

3.

Bottoms Up!

What's the difference between a toy poodle and a ferret? If you're a crooked pet dealer, not much besides some steroids and a perm.

In 2012, a retired Argentinian man took his two toy poodles to the local veterinarian. He had purchased the animals in Buenos Aires, but after returning home with them, he sensed that something might be off. Indeed, there was.

NUEVA MODALIDAD DE ESTAFA
¿CANICHE TOY O HURON?

His veterinarian informed him that his beloved toy poodles were actually giant ferrets. Apparently, some extra grooming and a steady diet of steroids were enough to make a bunch of juiced-up ferrets appear like miniature dogs. Another woman later came forward to reveal that she too had been tricked into buying what she thought was a chihuahua but was really another roid rodent.

Before we go blaming the customers, let's think about this from the perspective of cognitive science. There's an important distinction between what researchers refer to as *bottom-up* processing versus *top-down* processing. Bottom-up processing is perception built from the ground up. It is taking the various streams of sensory information that you are getting in the moment and using that information to form a coherent understanding or "representation." In the case of the ferrets on steroids, our bottom-up processing tells us that the monstrosity on the right side of the photo (previous page) has few of the features of a typical poodle. The eyes and nose are different; the ears aren't visible; poodles don't *hiss*.

Top-down processing, in contrast, is where our prior knowledge and expectations play a key role in what we are perceiving. Think about your prior beliefs, similar things you have seen in the past, what you expect based on the context. In the case of the ferrets, the customers who mistakenly purchased them thinking they were poodles likely experienced many top-down effects: The animals were advertised as poodles, they were probably sold in dog cages—few would suspect that the animals were really ferrets. The customers' prior expectations changed how they perceived the animals.

My point? When people set out to develop creative ideas, they often wind up with *ferrets on steroids*, meaning they have let their prior expectations, their top-down beliefs, dictate where they look for new ideas. However, as we'll see in this chapter, creative breakthroughs often come from letting the raw data—the bottom-up information—guide us to promising terrain.

Consider the story of Joanna Griffiths, an entrepreneur who built a successful global brand by taking a bottom-up approach. After university, Griffiths pursued an MBA where she had the thought of starting her own underwear brand, Knix. Like many women, she was frustrated by an industry that seemed to cater to men's idea of what women wanted rather than women's actual needs.

Griffiths used her time in business school as a learning lab. In one interview she said, "I did what is called digital anthropology, which is a fancy way of saying online creeping in chat rooms and forums. I was really just listening to what people were saying and being a part of the community and making people feel comfortable and safe enough to talk to me about some really personal and intimate things."

From this ear-to-the-ground approach, Griffiths identified an overlooked area of the market: leakproof underwear specifically designed for women postpartum and during menstruation. As the idea began to crystallize, she sought funding from investors.

But she was told that her idea was too niche and did not address a big enough problem, which she of course disagreed with: "And I mean, you have to look at this for what it is . . . we're talking about things that half of the population experiences, and through this narrow lens, I was being told that it was too niche of a market."

So, instead, Griffiths decided to raise capital using crowdfunding. During her Kickstarter campaign, the Hudson's Bay department store took interest and began ordering Knix underwear. By fall, shipments were going out to customers. Word spread, and within three years Knix underwear was available in over seven hundred stores and online. Shortly thereafter, Griffiths launched a second product, a seamless bra. It was wildly successful, bringing in over $1.3 million in just one month.

In 2022, Griffiths sold an 80% stake in Knix to a Swedish hygiene-product company, Essity, for the not-so-niche amount of $320 million.

Griffith's story tells us something important about the origins of successful ideas. By letting data, rather than other people's expectations, guide her approach, Griffiths identified an ignored area of possibility—not just for underwear but also for functional designs that actually addressed women's needs. She found opportunity in the negative space between existing ideas.

Our brains naturally pay attention to stuff, not the absence of it. This makes sense. If you're playing catch, it's the flying ball, not the space around it, that will cause injury. But a powerful source of creativity lies in paying attention to what's not there; what's missing.

Consider Alexander Fleming's discovery of antibiotics. While studying bacteria in his lab, he noticed something odd about one of his petri dishes—a spot where nothing was growing. That absence led him to investigate the mold contaminating his sample, which turned out to be penicillin, the world's first antibiotic.

Or take John Cage's famous piece *4'33"*, which instructs performers not to play their instruments during the entire piece. The piece draws awareness to everything that takes place during the "silence"— the shuffling of the musicians and audience, an occasional cough, one's own breathing and heartbeat, perhaps even faint auditory hallucinations. Written off by some critics as a gimmick, the idea of *4'33"* is quite profound; a seemingly simple gesture reminds us that we are never truly in silence.

We are often too eager to focus on what's already there, perhaps convinced that certain creative paths have been exhausted. But as Griffiths, Fleming, and Cage remind us, breakthrough ideas often emerge from the spaces in between—the gaps, absences, and silences that others overlook. Sometimes the most profound insights are discovered by noticing what isn't there.

Be a Problem Finder

One of the most challenging aspects of creativity isn't solving problems; it's finding them in the first place. When a creative problem is well defined, we know what we're aiming for and what rules to follow. We can tell if we're getting closer to a solution or veering off track. But identifying a new problem—seeing what others have missed—that's where many creative breakthroughs begin. In the example of Joanna Griffiths and Knix, the difficult part was not designing the product; it was figuring out what women needed to begin with.

In the 1960s, two psychologists—Mihaly Csikszentmihalyi and Jacob Getzels—conducted a fascinating study to understand how people engage in this kind of *problem finding* and how it impacts their long-term success. They recruited thirty-one visual artists from the prestigious Art Institute of Chicago. Then, one at a time, each of the artists was led into a studio furnished with two tables. On one table was a collection of objects that artists might typically use to create a still life: a leather-bound book, the gearshift for a car, a velvet hat, a prism . . . you know, *artsy stuff.* On the other table were drawing supplies, including paper, pencils, and charcoal.

The instructions were straightforward: Choose some objects from the first table, arrange them in any manner you like, then create a drawing. The artists were free to take as much time as they wanted, start over if they needed, and to stop only when they were satisfied with the outcome. The researchers' goal was to emulate a typical drawing setting as closely as possible, and indeed, the majority of the artists reported that they felt no different than in their daily practice.

While the artists were drawing, a member of the research team kept a written and photographic record of everything they observed. How many objects were selected; which objects; how unusual were they? How much time did the artist spend inspecting the objects before choosing them? How long did they spend arranging the objects? Then, after the artists completed their drawings, they were interviewed extensively in conversations that lasted up to four hours. During the interview the artists were asked to reconstruct their thought process: What went on in their minds when they began selecting the objects? What did they attend to or ignore? How did they evaluate the final product?

Answers to the questions were coded, and where possible, placed on a quantitative continuum. What Csikszentmihalyi and Getzels were most interested in was the amount and type of problem finding: To what extent did the artist come in with a preconceived notion about how they wanted to approach the drawing task versus experiment, play around with the objects, and in some sense, allow a problem to emerge from what they observed?

For example, one artist reported, "I knew right away I was going to make a drawing of a startling vanishing point." This approach scored on the lower end of the problem-finding scale. In contrast, another artist reported how they noticed shapes that were formed by the negative spaces in between objects and began experimenting with the forms that emerged from this perspective. This approach scored on the higher end of the problem-finding scale.

Then Csikszentmihalyi and Getzels waited. They waited seven years until 1970, when they checked in on the careers of the thirty-one artists in their study. The researchers interviewed art critics, gallery owners, and other known artists about what each of their participants were up to now. By this time, roughly half of the original cohort had either stopped producing art or their whereabouts were unknown. Among the other half, seven were still producing art with some success, and nine had already become rather well known—they were represented by leading galleries in Chicago and New York. One artist had already sold work to a museum. From these various indicators, Csikszentmihalyi and Getzels scored the relative success of each artist on a 10-point scale.

This process was repeated once again in 1981, now eighteen years after the original study. By that time, some of the participants had become unqualified "stars," whose work was internationally recognized, regularly shown in the world's top museums and galleries.

What predicted success? The artists who talked about drive or ambition were not the ones who were successful later. Nor was it the ones who opined generally on the importance of seeking "beauty," or "order," or "harmony." It wasn't the artists who seemed confident, nor was it the ones who had worked out a deep, philosophical approach to their artistic practice.

Instead, it was the problem finders. And not just any type of problem finding. The most successful artists were the ones who engaged in problem finding at the very beginning of the task. They were the artists who approached the drawing task without any preconceived notions—or at least, none that they expressed—and allowed the shape and structure of their still life to emerge from the situation itself. And it wasn't just what those artists said. The most successful artists also explored and manipulated the objects much more than the rest.

When you think about it, the results of this study are really quite astounding. Subtle differences in how a group of art students approached a single drawing task predicted career outcomes nearly twenty years later. And this result is even more impressive when you consider that the researchers did not factor in any visual elements about the drawings, such as artistic skill or composition. It was merely what the artists communicated about problem finding—whether they approached the creative task with preexisting expectations or instead allowed their drawing to emerge, bottom-up.

The lesson here isn't just for artists. Successful creatives of many types benefit from problem finding. Whether it's the entrepreneur who begins generating business ideas by observing potential customers, the scientist who hunts for unexpected results, or the journalist who digs for inconsistencies—success comes when we look beyond the obvious and allow creative directions to emerge naturally from the environment. When we pay close attention to our surroundings, new opportunities and challenges begin to reveal themselves. Our task then is to learn to recognize these signals—to understand that creativity isn't about forcing solutions but about uncovering what's already there.

Practice Close Looking

How do we look past our expectations to see what is really in front of us? One powerful strategy, which comes from world of art history, is the practice of *close looking*. Close looking is a deliberate and attentive examination of an object—for example, a painting or sculpture—with great detail and focus. It involves slowing down and devoting time to explore the nuances that may often go unnoticed at first glance. You might spend thirty minutes or even an hour looking at a single painting.

Similar to meditation, when you first practice close looking, your mind will race. Looking at a painting, for example, your inner explainer might scream, *Okay, okay, I get it already. There's a house. There's a woman. Let's move on!* But sit with the image for a minute, and new details emerge. You begin to draw connections between different elements of the painting and begin to form theories about what the artist might have been trying to communicate through their choices.

For years, I have taught seminars with business executives where we talk about leadership and how to communicate one's values in the workplace. Sometimes these conversations went swimmingly, but other times they fell flat. Then I got the idea to precede our conversation with a trip to the art museum. With the help of experienced and insightful docents, we would spend an hour practicing close looking—focusing on one or two pictures for the entire time and discussing what we saw.

Initially, the executives were a bit hesitant to engage in the exercise. Perhaps they were worried about appearing like they "didn't get it." Soon, though, the floodgates would open. They started noticing different subtle elements in the painting and began making all kinds of interesting connections to their own lives. What had at first seemed like a foreign and slightly awkward exercise became one of the highlights of the weeklong experience.

But the most remarkable aspect of the close-looking exercise did not take place in the art museum; rather, it was the effect that it had on our conversations once we returned to the classroom. Not only were the executives more engaged, but they now began to use close looking in their approach to leadership. By scrutinizing their interactions and even seemingly mundane meetings, they noticed new details and subtleties in their behavior. They drew new and different connections and understood what their actions communicated in a different light. They were better able to look past a simplified representation of their behaviors, to see what was *really* there. Close looking led them to new, unexplored terrain.

The beauty of close looking is that it's available to all of us, at any moment. You might start with something simple like spending ten minutes really observing how your work team reacts when someone presents an idea, or by observing how customers peruse items in your store, or by noticing the steps you take when performing daily tasks like getting ready in the morning or winding down at night. Let yourself notice each behavior, the frictions, the patterns or connections between events. What starts as a passive exercise in observation can often be a powerful catalyst to identify where change is needed and where there are untapped opportunities. The more you practice this kind of deep attention, the more natural it becomes—and the more likely you are to spot a new creative problem when it emerges.

Cultivate a Knowledge Funnel

In the beginning of the book, we explored how expertise shapes our ability to recognize promising ideas. Deep knowledge in a domain helps us understand what promising ideas look like and where others have found success. Without this foundation, creative exploration becomes mere guesswork.

But the message of this chapter is different—it's about seeing the world with fresh eyes. Let go of your expectations and try to see what's really there. By doing so, we allow new creative directions to emerge—bottom-up—becoming problem finders. This seems to suggest that extensive knowledge in a domain may do more harm than good.

So, which is it? How can expertise be both essential to discovery and potentially a hinderance?

First, it is important to recognize that the extensive knowledge we accumulate about a topic or field is different from what we may notice in the moment when we are embarking on a new creative venture. If we're not careful, that prior knowledge can seep in and distort our judgment, as we saw with the "ferrets on steroids" example. But it doesn't have to. We *can* focus on what's in front of us, practice close looking, and attend to the negative spaces. We can, to the best of our ability, remain in the moment and attentive when searching for promising new ideas.

In short, learn extensively about your area of interest and how others found success. Then try to put that inner explainer to the side when you are actually "in the field," searching for new creative problems.

Second, the most successful creatives I know have a striking thing in common: They have developed a *knowledge funnel*. They know a lot about one or two things and a little about a lot of things. But more than just that, they are highly adept at relating those foreign ideas back to their own expertise. Great visual artists will take concepts from philosophy or science and translate them into their preferred medium. Great musicians can take ideas from completely different musical genres or totally different arts and connect those ideas back to their own instrument. Great chefs might find inspiration from ideas totally unrelated to food or cooking. And some of the most successful scientists I know can take a concept from some distant field, translate it into the language of their own expertise, and see the implications for a problem they are working on.

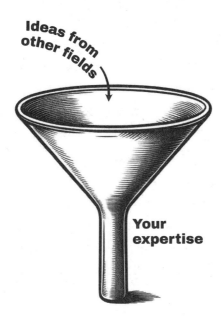

The knowledge funnel is about more than just accumulating knowledge and exposure to new things. Someone with this ability has formed a deep understanding of what successful ideas look like in their own area. This allows them to quickly understand the promise of new ideas and how those ideas might impact their work. At the same time, they are constantly searching, trying to expand outward, looking to connect what they know in new and different ways. Curiosity, close looking, and in-the-moment attentiveness are essential—but so is the ability to understand the implications of those new ideas for your own expertise.

Consider the work of physician and author Alice Flaherty. Flaherty is a neurologist at Massachusetts General Hospital and faculty at Harvard Medical School. Following the tragic loss of her twin boys, who were born prematurely and died shortly after birth, Flaherty was gripped with a rare condition known as hypergraphia, which is the overwhelming compulsion to write. For four months, she wrote non-stop. She recalled, "My writing *felt* like a disease: I could not stop, and it sucked me away from family and friends. Sensations outside of language dried up: music became irritating discord, the visual world grew faint. . . . [It] also felt like one of the best things that has ever happened to me. It still does."

This led Flaherty to become interested in the biological basis of creativity—what turns it on and what can block it. In her research, Flaherty examined the lives of famous creatives throughout history. Then, given her medical expertise, she began to interpret these historical cases through the lens of neurology, given what is known about these individuals and the medical conditions that impacted them. The result was *The Midnight Disease*, a book that offers many fresh insights into the brain structures implicated in creativity and the delicate balance between them.

For example, Flaherty documents many successful authors throughout history who have suffered from temporal lobe epilepsy: Fyodor Dostoevsky, Lewis Carroll, Gustave Flaubert, Edgar Allan Poe, among others. She also discusses how many celebrated writers and artists, like Sylvia Plath, Ernest Hemingway, F. Scott Fitzgerald, Charles Dickens, Charles Ives, Charlie Parker, Georgia O'Keeffe, and Virginia Woolf have suffered from bipolar disorder. In fact, writers are ten times more likely to experience manic-depressive episodes than the rest of the population, and poets are nearly forty times more likely.

And the fascinating part of these particular neurological correlates of creativity is that they are entirely consistent with the main thesis of this book: Creativity is about discovery.

Let me explain: Temporal lobe epilepsy and bipolar disorder are conditions that primarily affect emotion and drive. So it's not as if there is some inner seed of creativity—some wellspring of ideas—that magically becomes unlocked by these conditions. Rather, seizures, mania, and traumatic events can lead to a sudden surge in emotional drive and one's search for meaning, which leads people to engage in creative exploration—generating copious amounts of material, finding new and far-afield connections, and hunting for solutions to vexing creative problems. As Flaherty put it, "In psychological terms, it seems that drive is more important than talent."

Creative breakthroughs do not come from choosing between expertise and fresh eyes but from learning to use both. And the knowledge funnel is a practical tool that allows us to do this. It allows us to see both the forest and the trees, revealing new creative directions and possibilities. As you develop your own knowledge funnel, remember to dive deep but keep your peripheral vision wide. This is how we identify promising new sites for creative excavation.

Exercises

This chapter is about problem finding and letting the data, rather than your preconceived notions, guide you. Since this is mostly a matter of perception and attention to detail, the exercises below are intended to enhance your ability to look at your environment and think about the world in a bottom-up way.

Exercise 9: Silent Spaces in Conversations

The goal of this exercise is to identify the significance of what is *not said* in conversations. In your next few conversations, pay close attention to pauses and silences, and what is left unsaid by the other person. (Note: best to do this with a family member or close friend. Carefully attending to the negative spaces might make you act a little "off," so avoid practicing this in an important meeting or interview.)

- **Start by simply noticing the cadence of the person's pauses and silences.** Are they frequent or infrequent? How long do the pauses last? Is there a rhythm to them?

- **Notice the context in which the pauses occur.** Is it only when the person catches their breath; is it only when they are really thinking or saying something more abstract? What else do you notice during those pauses? Does the person close their eyes or avert their gaze? Do they touch their face or change their posture?

- **Now think about what is happening in the person's mind during those silences.** Are they thinking about what they just said? Are they thinking about what they will say next? Are they pausing to study your behavior?

- **Finally, form a theory** about how the negative spaces shaped your perceptions of the person and the conversation. Did the person seem relaxed? Excited? Disengaged?

- **Debrief.** Tell the person about your theories (and perhaps why you have been acting so weird in the conversation). Were your theories accurate regarding what they were thinking and feeling during those silences?

Exercise 10: Finding Problems in Daily Life

The goal of this exercise is to develop the skill of identifying unnoticed problems in everyday life.

- **For one week, carry a notebook** (or you can take notes on a mobile device). Document instances where you notice friction, or inconvenience, or inefficiency in your daily activities.

- **Review your notes** and identify themes or recurring issues. Highlight what seems most pervasive or impactful.

- **Choose one problem** you've identified and generate a list of potential solutions, no matter how outlandish.

- **Share your proposed solutions** with friends or colleagues for their insights. This can help refine your understanding of the problem and its possible solutions.

- **Challenge:** Based on your identification of problems from week 1, make predictions about the next week. Which of the same frictions will arise again? Implement a minor tweak and see if it makes a difference.

Exercise 11: How Negative Spaces Change Our Perception

This is a visual exercise to cultivate the ability to attend to the negative space in your environment and notice how differences in negative spaces influence your perception.

- **Take a smartphone or camera** and go to any location of your choice.

- **Choose a static scene**—in nature, an urban environment, or indoors—where the objects in your photo don't move for several minutes.

- **Take several photographs** of the same scene from different vantage points and perspectives. Crouch down. Shift to the side. Zoom in and out. Take at least ten photos.

- **Select two of the photos**—the same scene, but from different vantage points. Ideally, the two of the photos should make you feel slightly different things. Maybe one photo reminds you of a particular person or situation, while the other photo reminds you of something else.

- **Now pay attention to the negative spaces**. Take one of the photos and go through each region, carefully noticing the negative spaces that exist in between each of the objects. Imagine that the photo is an entirely flat, two-dimensional surface and each negative space is a shape. If you like, practice drawing only the negative spaces within the photo, or use photo-editing software to remove all the objects, leaving only the negative space.

- **Repeat this process** for the other photo you selected.

- **Compare the negative spaces** across the photos you selected. How are the shapes defined by the negative spaces changing and morphing from one photo to the next? How do the colors of the negative space change? How do the sizes of the different negative spaces relative to the objects change? Notice how the difference in negative space changes what the photo makes you feel and think about.

Exercise 12: Object Storytelling

This exercise is inspired by a fantastic book called *Significant Objects* by Joshua Glenn and Rob Walker. The goal is to apply close looking to everyday objects to imagine their history.

- **Select an everyday object** that you find interesting. The object should be used, with some visible wear and tear; something you borrowed, something you purchased at a secondhand store, or something that you found. If you're on an airplane, it could be safety instructions in the seat back in front of you.

- **Spend time examining the object closely.** Note its design, materials, wear patterns, and any marks or inscriptions.

- **Now close your eyes and focus solely on the sense of touch.** Note the feelings and impressions each texture evokes.

- **Think about what the object was like** when it was brand-new and note every new detail or marking it acquired during its history.

- **Begin to create an imaginary story** about the events that produced each of those markings. What was the history of the object? How was it handled or used? What was the person like who made these markings on it?

SURVEYING: THE BIG TAKEAWAYS

The main idea in Surveying is that before you can embark on your creative journey, you first need to identify which part of the landscape you want to explore. This should be a topic or creative pursuit that thrills you. If you don't love the journey, you will never make it to your destination.

But there's more to it than just that.

- **Let go of your inner genius.** Burn the cabin down. If you are feeling stuck, remember to reorient and look outward. Forget about yourself and what your creative output says about you. Allow curiosity to be your guide.

- **Put originality on pause.** One of the best places to find a successful idea is next to other great ideas. Start by emulating a hero. Do a deep dive on a specific topic and step inside your hero's mind. Add sprinkles of novelty as you make it your own. Remember the spark of creativity often begins with what's new and exciting to you, not necessarily what's new to everyone.

- **Take a bottom-up approach.** Let the data guide you. Practice close looking and attend to the negative spaces. Allow problems to emerge from what you notice. Think about cultivating a knowledge funnel as you relate far-afield ideas back to your own expertise.

PART II

Gridding

In music, I've done tons of formal experimentation.
It's the same way painters do, the same way
writers do, where I've started with a technical idea,
and it's a jigsaw puzzle I'm putting together.
I don't just come from this raw, emotional state.

—KATHLEEN HANNA, musician and author,
Bikini Kill, Le Tigre, the Julie Ruin

Personally, I'm not the biggest fan of "systematic steps." My desk is a disaster zone of books and Post-it Notes with illegible scribbles. I have difficulty following recipes. I often throw out the instructions with the box. If you're someone who groans at the thought of making your creativity systematic and organized, you are not alone.

But in this section, we'll see why approaching creativity in an organized way is so powerful. For example, consider the results of an impressive experiment that followed real entrepreneurs as they developed and launched their own businesses. Half of the entrepreneurs were randomly assigned to take a "scientific approach" as they searched for potential business ideas, while the other half developed ideas more haphazardly. In the end, being organized paid off: The entrepreneurs who used an organized method for generating ideas considered more ideas, were more selective, and ultimately went on to create more successful businesses than those who did not. And this isn't just true in business. Thinking systematically—like a scientist (or archeologist)—can be incredibly effective in everything from art to design to literature to entertainment.

In archeology, gridding is the process of sectioning off an area for excavation. Once an archaeologist has identified an area of interest—often through historical records and preliminary surveys—the next step is to create a grid system for detailed examination and recording.

To make a grid, the archeologist uses twine or string stretched between stakes across the site, dividing it into smaller, manageable squares. Each grid square is explored, and the location of any found object is recorded. This step ensures that the excavation is well organized and no part of the site is overlooked. It lets the archeologist know where they found things, and equally, where they didn't.

Similar to how archaeologists use physical grids to map and explore physical space, in this section we'll discuss strategies for Gridding your conceptual space. The idea is to map your brainstorming space, providing a way of carefully searching through it, and making sure that every combination of elements is explored.

In this section we'll learn about the *guiding question* that serves as our compass, helping us to orient and find creative direction. We'll also discuss the *grid* itself, which is a tool that helps us to identify the boundaries of creative problem and the various combinations of ideas that exist within that space. And we'll learn about *transplanting*, which is a method of importing ideas from one creative field to another, allowing you to cross-pollinate ideas from seemingly different domains.

But not to worry, it will still be fun! What makes creativity deeply pleasurable is that you are engrossed in the task. You lose a sense of time and maybe even place. You enter what Mihaly Csikszentmihalyi called a "flow state."

What I have noticed is that using the tools of Gridding and allowing my mind to go down one line of thought and then the next—exploring each possibility—is equally as engrossing, and equally as flow-inducing, as if I were to jump around from one idea to the next. The major difference is that by using Gridding, I bother to check every nook and cranny for ideas, often leaving me much more to work with in the end.

4.

The Guiding Question

By his late twenties, Danny Meyer was already a force in New York's fine-dining scene. He opened the famed Union Square Cafe when he was only twenty-seven and quickly followed it with other hit restaurants like Gramercy Tavern and the Modern.

In 2001, Meyer was approached by his friend Susan Freedman, who ran a nonprofit arts organization called the Public Art Fund. The organization was putting together a new exhibit, *Target Art in the Park*, which was designed to invigorate Madison Square Park through public-focused art. "We had this artist Navin Rawanchaikul who did a project, *I Love Taxi*, and it was important to him to have a food component. And there was only one logical place to go, and that was to Danny [Meyer)]," Freedman recalled.

At the time, Meyer had several high-end restaurants, including Eleven Madison Park, which was located only a block away from Madison Square Park. The three-starred Michelin restaurant included exotic items like foie gras, sweetbreads, and sea urchin. *The New York Times* once referred to Eleven Madison Park as "among the most alluring and impressive restaurants in New York."

Meyer's contribution to the art project? Hot dogs.

"There was this artist from Thailand and he had this idea called I Heart Taxi, I Love Taxi, with these cartoonlike taxi cabs on stilts," Meyer said. "We had a kitchen that was not being used that much upstairs at Eleven Madison Park at that time, and we said, well, we'll make the hot dogs. . . . Everyone told me, you're absolutely crazy to be doing a hot-dog cart."

The hot-dog cart was intended to be a one-off, but then 9/11 happened. "The city went into both an emotional and financial depression. And the following summer, 2002, the community said, can we please bring back the hot-dog cart because it made us happy, even though there would be new art in the park. So, we brought it back. And we did it for a third year, in 2003."

The hot-dog cart became so popular that Meyer went to the city to request a permanent kiosk. He promised to add other crowd favorites like cheeseburgers, milkshakes, and French fries. Meyer's request was granted, and he enlisted the help of his longtime friend and business partner Randy Garutti.

Meyer and Garutti envisioned a modern version of a roadside burger stand. Their idea wasn't about replicating the past; in fact, both Meyer and Garutti disliked the gimmick of the '50s diner. Rather, their idea was about capturing the essence of what made classic burger stands great. Their initial menu included recognizable items like burgers, crinkle-cut fries, and frozen custard but also featured experiments that didn't make the final cut, such as tuna burgers and espresso. Even the name Shake Shack wasn't immediately obvious. They contemplated names like Madison Mixer, Custard Park, and Dog Run (woof!).

Flash-forward twenty years. The modest hot-dog cart transformed into a multibillion-dollar company with over four hundred locations worldwide. But how does such a transformation happen? How does an art project become Shake Shack, a global phenomenon?

Step 1: Explore Familiar Ground

Meyer's years running fine-dining restaurants taught him that success isn't just about execution; it's about choosing the right thing to execute in the first place. When the hot-dog cart struck a chord with New Yorkers, Meyer recognized an opportunity to take American classics and elevate them. No gimmicks, just the essentials, done remarkably well. He was showing how something familiar could become exceptional.

What makes this approach to creativity so powerful is that it combines a foundation of proven ground with the thrill of discovery. Yes, people already loved burgers and shakes. But Meyer knew there was still room to explore—to find that sweet spot. Recall the "5% novelty" principle discussed in Chapter 2, where tiny changes to established concepts can create something remarkable and new. Meyer searched in terrain he understood, looking for those crucial differences that would set Shake Shack apart.

This is where Meyer's expertise really mattered: not just in knowing how to run restaurants, but in knowing that this creative path was worth pursuing.

Step 2: Test and Learn

As Meyer and Garutti refined the Shake Shack concept, they relied heavily on experimentation and trial and error. The team tried every imaginable combination and ratio of ingredients. They took copious notes, documenting the results as each element was tested. Meyer applied the same care and scrutiny to perfecting a $5 hamburger as he did the $50 entrees in his high-end restaurants.

For example, in 2012, Shake Shack was reviewed by *New York Times* food critic Pete Wells. Wells gave them only one star. He said some nice things about the burger and shake, but he had one major critique: "Mr. Meyer runs one of the world's great restaurant companies. Can't one of his chefs show him how to make a decent French fry?"

Wells's concern was that the fries were made from frozen potatoes. "Freezing turns them mealy, and no amount of oil or salt can make them taste like the fresh-cut potatoes that are standard issue at some burger joints now."

Most owners of a burger stand would have shrugged it off. *"Okay, so the food critic from the* Times *doesn't like our fries? Big deal. Who gives a shack?"* But in the world of fine dining, a review from *The New York Times* can make or break a career.

So Meyer set out to find the perfect French fry. He flew around the country inspecting potato farms and meeting with different farmers. He and his team experimented with different shapes, thicknesses, amounts of frying, types of oil, duration in the oil, and amount of salt. He even found a farmer who was willing to measure the sugar content of the potatoes before sending them. The team collected copious amounts of data about how much people enjoyed the taste and experience of eating different versions of the fries. They gathered ratings from their staff, focus groups, and actual trials in their restaurants.

Ironically, after spending months and a small fortune, it turned out that the perfect fry wasn't a fresh fry at all. It was frozen. To customers, the frozen fry is the fry from their childhoods—the essence of what a fry should be.

Some might say Meyer overshot in his pursuit of the "perfect fry." But his creative journey had revealed something deeper. He wasn't necessarily looking for the best-tasting fry. He was looking for the fry that captured people's imaginations and sense of nostalgia.

Step 3: Have a Guiding Question

A frozen fry probably isn't going to be people's favorite in all contexts. It might not even be the option that objectively tastes the best (as the critic Pete Wells pointed out). Yet it was perfect for what Shake Shack was trying to accomplish.

But how did Meyer and his team know what they were looking for? How do you take an initial spark of an idea and figure out where to explore? This comes from having a *guiding question.*

A guiding question is like a compass, clarifying your goal and helping you recognize when you've achieved it. It comes from considering two key things: *what* you are trying to accomplish and *why* that is important or meaningful to people. Instead of wandering aimlessly, having a guiding question points you in a particular creative direction.

Let's consider Shake Shack's guiding question, which I would phrase like this:

What is a restaurant that captures the essence of an American burger stand and appeals to people's sense of nostalgia, without feeling gimmicky?

Why is this a successful guiding question? For starters, it is *specific*. It tells us about the kind of food, and the feeling the business is trying to capture. Second, it is *open-ended*. Working within this general space, there are lots of different forms the restaurant could take. Third, it is *motivating*. Although the general terrain of burgers and fries is well known, for Meyer and Garutti, there was excitement around early success and a desire to better understand what about that experience resonated with people. And it is *measurable*. They can look at customer reviews, focus groups, and customer surveys. All of these measures provided important data to figure out if they were on the right track.

A guiding question isn't just useful for restaurants. Writers use guiding questions to shape stories, scientists use them to frame research, designers use them to develop products, and entrepreneurs use them to build businesses. Even for smaller projects like developing a presentation for work or tackling a school project, a guiding question can transform a vague creative vision into focused and systematic exploration.

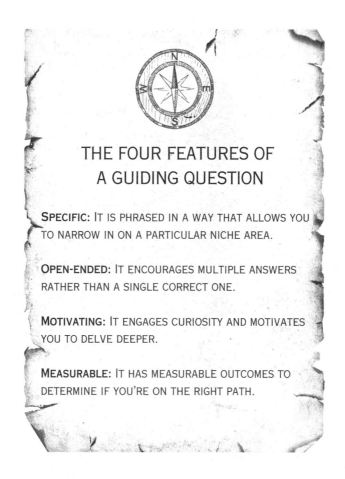

THE FOUR FEATURES OF A GUIDING QUESTION

SPECIFIC: IT IS PHRASED IN A WAY THAT ALLOWS YOU TO NARROW IN ON A PARTICULAR NICHE AREA.

OPEN-ENDED: IT ENCOURAGES MULTIPLE ANSWERS RATHER THAN A SINGLE CORRECT ONE.

MOTIVATING: IT ENGAGES CURIOSITY AND MOTIVATES YOU TO DELVE DEEPER.

MEASURABLE: IT HAS MEASURABLE OUTCOMES TO DETERMINE IF YOU'RE ON THE RIGHT PATH.

How to Develop a Guiding Question

Many successful artists report that their creative process begins with a guiding question, or at least, something like it—a specific feeling, or mood, or setting that they want to capture, though not necessarily a clear path about how to get there.

In Adam Moss's *The Work of Art*, in which he interviews successful artists, poets, and filmmakers, the idea of a guiding question repeatedly emerges. The poet Louise Glück, for example, often works from assignments that her friends and fellow poets give her. She describes how a specific prompt like "write a poem that contains an invitation" can be a powerful engine for creative discovery.

Filmmaker Sofia Coppola discusses how the creative spark for making *Lost in Translation* was a specific fantasy that involved getting a drink with the actor Bill Murray: "It really just started with Tokyo," Coppola said. "I was newly married when I would go there, and I was not feeling connected in my marriage. So, I was lonely and drifting, and it was just sort of a fantasy that Bill Murray would show up at the bar. And I mean, really Bill Murray. I wrote it for him, and I wasn't going to make it without him."

These examples show how guiding questions emerge organically in creative work. But I've found that actually putting pen to paper and deliberately crafting a guiding question can make your creative process dramatically more focused and effective. Below is a template that captures the key elements of what we've discussed.

Guiding Question Template:

"What is a [type of project] that [provides a unique form of value or meaning] for [a particular audience] in [a specific context/ environment], despite [potential obstacles]?"

[Type of project]: Specify the kind of idea, or object, or experience you aim to create.

[Unique Value]: Describe the importance or meaning that your idea provides. *Why* should it exist? This should include some details that are relevant to what sets the idea apart and makes it unique.

[Audience]: Define *who* will benefit from or be interested in the idea. Why will this group, in particular, recognize its importance or meaning?

[Context]: Describe where and how your idea will be experienced.

[Obstacles]: Acknowledge specific challenges you might face.

When you first begin drafting your guiding question, you may not know the answers to all of these questions; that's fine. However, the more precise you can be, the better.

We've discussed Shake Shack, but let's consider another example of how a guiding question can look.

In the mid-1960s, Marie Van Brittan Brown had a specific challenge. Living in Jamaica, Queens, Brown confronted a reality that many New Yorkers faced at that time: high crime rates and slow police response times. As a nurse working irregular hours, Brown often returned home late at night or in the early morning. Her husband, an electronics technician, also worked odd shifts, leaving her alone at home for long stretches.

Each time someone knocked on her door, Brown froze. There was no way to safely see who was there. Peepholes could be easily covered, and opening the door meant exposing herself to whatever waited outside. With police response times in her neighborhood stretching past an hour, she couldn't afford to guess wrong.

Brown decided to design her own peace of mind. We might phrase her guiding question like this:

What is a home monitoring system that allows a single person to safely screen visitors, without needing to open the door?

Patent US3482037A to Marie Van Brittan Brown and Albert L Brown, Home security system utilizing television surveillance (1969).

Working with her husband Albert's electronics expertise, Brown developed an elaborate system of peepholes at different heights on her front door, paired with a sliding, motorized camera that could peer through them. The camera connected to a monitor inside her home, letting her see visitors clearly from her bedroom. She added two-way microphones for communication, allowing her to question whoever came to her door. For emergencies, she even devised a way to alert police by radio.

Brown's guiding question led to the first home security system, which she patented in 1969. Today, many features we take for granted in security systems—video doorbells, remote monitoring, two-way communication—can be traced back to her original design. By clearly defining what she was trying to achieve and why it mattered for the people who would use it, Brown was able to develop something truly innovative.

An interesting wrinkle in Brown's story is that the security system that she and her husband developed never made it into production. It was simply too expensive. But that reveals another important feature of guiding questions: They're dynamic, not static. They often start broad and become more focused as you gather information, test ideas, and gain new insights. The question evolves as you come to better understand what you're searching for. In fact, refining your guiding question is very much a part of the creative process itself.

Even though Brown's particular version of the idea did not land, the broader principles did. Others were able to focus further on the conceptual terrain that she identified.

Take an Outside-In Perspective

For many academics—me included—teaching does not come naturally. Most professors don't receive any formal training in teaching as part of their graduate studies, and in many cases, their own niche area of research is too specific to have much application in the classroom. So it's a real challenge to create a course that is informative, engaging, and accessible for students. For some, teaching appears effortless and natural. But in my experience, the professors who make it look easy are the ones who have spent countless hours planning, pruning, and refining.

Before designing specific course content—like selecting readings and laying out the curriculum—a professor needs to make many choices: What topics am I going to focus on for this lecture? Or, more generally, what is this course going to be about? These are opportunities for a guiding question.

Over time, I have found that the success of a lecture, and the success of the course overall, depends a lot on the method that I use to formulate the guiding question for my course.

When I first began teaching, I defaulted to what I'll call the *inside-out method*. This is how people typically approach lots of creative endeavors. They begin by considering their own goals and aspirations. They think about what they want to say or communicate and lay out a plan for achieving it. In teaching, for example, I considered what I thought was relevant and important for students to know—often colored by what I found personally interesting—and began to narrow in that way. The results of this method? Not great.

Then I essentially started from scratch, reversing my process entirely. Before even beginning to develop specific course content, I tried to imagine my students at the end of the semester. What kinds of things would they find informative and impactful? What would they potentially take away with them or remember years down the road? I call this the *outside-in method*.

The starting point of the outside-in method is the anticipated experience of people engaging with the final work. You take the perspective of someone who is, for example, taking your class, experiencing your art, reading your book, or using your product, and imagine how they will receive it when it's all said and done. This method involves cultivating an understanding of the audience's needs, their desires, and potential reactions. To take an outside-in perspective, you have to let go of your own ambitions and instead imagine the various ways in which a person will interact with and be impacted by your work.

When I considered my classes from this outside-in perspective, a very different guiding question emerged. Rather than starting with my research interests in psychology, I began imagining my students five years after graduation. What concepts would they still reference? What frameworks would help them understand new challenges? What skills would make them more effective in their chosen paths?

This shift produced immediate, practical changes in how I designed my course. Topics and "classic findings" that I had taught for a decade or longer were cut overnight. Instead of diving deep into theoretical frameworks that fascinated me, I started each unit with real-world applications—the lectures were focused on the practical problems that my students face every day. And if I referenced an experiment or real-life example, it was to highlight the ways in which it might challenge their current thinking and worldview.

What I realized by taking the outside-in perspective was that scientific concepts and theories are useful to *me* because that is what *I* do every day. But if I didn't provide my students with a way to slot those ideas into their immediate needs and questions—their day-to-day—they were likely to forget the information almost as quickly as they learned it.

This outside-in approach extends far beyond the classroom. Consider an entrepreneur developing a new product. Instead of starting with their innovative idea and pushing it forward, they might begin by trying to understand their customers' frustrations and unmet needs. Or, an artist might begin by envisioning their audience's journey as they walk through the gallery or sit through a performance, rather than by focusing on their own artistic vision or the piece itself.

The power of the outside-in method lies in its ability to transform creative blocks into opportunities. When a writer feels stuck, they can shift from asking, "What do I want to say?" to "What does my reader need to hear?" Or a public speaker preparing for a presentation can move beyond "What information do I need to cover?" to "What will my audience be thinking about on their drive home?" This subtle shift in focus often unleashes new creative possibilities.

But be sure to test your intuitions. Some of your hunches about your audience will be correct. Many may not be. Share your guiding question with potential audience members and be sure to ask them what they think. Their reactions and feedback can reveal important blind spots in your thinking.

The process of developing a guiding question is not unlike spotting the faint twinkle of something promising in the distance and then directing yourself toward it. Once something has captured your attention, begin to collect data and zero in. And don't be afraid to step outside yourself. Imagine the realization of your efforts and specifically who will receive them. What would they find especially persuasive or moving? Even in the earliest stages of developing your project, this sort of perspective can be a powerful way of reorienting your creative focus.

Exercises

These exercises are designed to help with formulating and refining a guiding question. As you're developing your guiding question, remember to focus on making it specific, open-ended, motivating, and measurable.

Exercise 13: The Elevator Pitch

The term "elevator pitch" is rumored to have originated in Hollywood when young screenwriters would wait for producers to enter the elevator at a major studio to tell them about their latest movie idea. But beyond just pitching movies, the notion of distilling your idea down to the essential *what* (the idea is) and *why* (it is useful) can be extremely helpful in formulating and refining your guiding question. The goal of this exercises is to explain your guiding question in the time it would take to ride an elevator (about one minute).

- **Start by describing your creative project.** What is it and who is it for?

- **Cut it down.** Chances are that the first thing you wrote or said aloud was way too long. How can you pair it down to the most essential elements?

- **Make your pitch compelling and understandable.** If you find yourself using jargon or specialized terminology, start over. Explain it in a way that appeals to what a person on the street would understand. Even better, try giving your pitch for real with someone else.

- **Focus on the why.** People's tendency, I've found, is to focus on the "what"—the kind of thing it is or other topics that are related. What often gets overlooked is the much more important question: "Why?" What problem is your idea trying to solve? (Recall our discussions from chapter 3 on the importance of problem finding.) Instead, I recommend starting with the problem—i.e., "The thing I/we are really trying to solve is," or "What has puzzled me and kept me awake at night is . . ."

- **Be prepared to change your idea.** Take notice of how you feel giving your elevator pitch. Are you bored (or embarrassed) before you finish? This has definitely happened to me, and if it happens to you, think about how you could tweak your idea to overcome those feelings. Over time, I've found that the elevator pitch can be an incredibly effective early-stage exercise for identifying the aspects of a project that I'm less excited about.

Exercise 14: The Olio Game

Olio is a Spanish stew, which literally translates to "rotten pot." The term is often used to refer to a mix of ingredients—a hodgepodge of ideas or elements brought together. This is a game that I developed to encourage thinking about how different types of things interact with different needs and purposes.

In the figure, you'll find a list of "ingredients" and a list of "twists." Select one ingredient and one twist. Then try to think of ideas that satisfy the prompt that you've created. If possible, try to make the pairings random to enhance the fun and surprise element. For example, you could roll dice once to select an ingredient and once again to select a twist. You can try this exercise alone, or you can play with other people, giving them prompts as a fresh challenge:

Example prompt: What is a [new theme park attraction] [that grandmothers will love]?

INGREDIENTS

1. new superhero
2. new musical instrument
3. new festival or celebration
4. new theme park attraction
5. new type of energy drink
6. new game or pastime
7. new kitchen gadget
8. new piece of furniture
9. new style of dance
10. new status symbol
11. new collectible item
12. new workout routine

TWISTS

1. that belongs in a rap video
2. that will go viral on social media
3. that is very romantic
4. that teachers will hate
5. that grandmothers will love
6. that doctors will recommend
7. that will cause arguments at parties
8. that won't be allowed by TSA
9. that will be lame to teenagers
10. that only artists will understand
11. that children will find hilarious
12. that only introverts will enjoy

Exercise 15: Refining Your Guiding Question

I'm always amazed by how much I can learn by putting even a vague crumb of an idea out there, and how powerful the initial feedback can be in helping me refine my guiding question. The goal of this exercise is to help you think about the questions you might ask to refine your guiding question. Gathering feedback could include talking with friends or colleagues, running a focus group, or something more elaborate, like a survey or experiment. The important part is to get a sense early on about how other people understand your idea. Note that chapter 12 provides several additional suggestions for how to collect feedback and learn from it.

Present your guiding question to someone else, then ask:

1. What does this question make you think of?
2. Can you think of an example (a product, a piece of art, a book) that already addresses this question? If so, what is it?
3. Does this question clearly define what the goal is? If not, what's missing?
4. Who do you think this question is most relevant to? Who would benefit from it?
5. What specific need or gap does this question address?
6. Does this question feel compelling or urgent to you?
7. Does this question suggest a clear next step? If you were pursuing this question yourself, where would you start?
8. What potential obstacles does this question overlook? What does this question miss?
9. Could this question be reframed to be more surprising or provocative? If so, how?

- **Once you gather some data**, think about how you can further refine your guiding question.

5.

Think Inside the Box

Henri Matisse had some of his greatest artistic epiphanies from his sickbed. The first occurred when, as a young man, he suffered a ruptured appendix. His mother brought him some art supplies so that he could occupy himself while he recovered. When he was well again, Matisse announced that he was abandoning his legal career to pursue his newfound passion for art. However, it would not be the last time that illness profoundly changed the nature and trajectory of Matisse's work.

After leaving his job as a law clerk, Matisse moved to Paris to attend art school. His earliest paintings were realistic and rather conservative. But over time, his work became more abstract as Matisse sought to "discover" the true nature of his subjects. His own style culminated in what would be known as Fauvism, characterized by bold colors and exaggerated forms. For the next forty years, Matisse enjoyed a great deal of professional success. His work was shown in leading galleries and exhibitions throughout the world.

Then, at the age of seventy-one, Matisse was diagnosed with abdominal cancer. To save his life, the doctors performed a dramatic operation that involved removing a significant portion of his intestines. While the surgery was considered a success, Matisse was left practically bedridden. The severity of the operation meant that Matisse could no longer stand for long periods, which was necessary for traditional canvas painting.

Matisse then began experimenting with an entirely new medium using paper cutouts. He would direct his assistants to paint paper with various colors and would cut shapes directly from these colored scraps. Initially, the cutouts were intended as preparatory works—studies for when his physical stamina returned. But over time, they evolved into an art form of their own. Matisse could now shape the color directly, without the need to use a paintbrush or canvas. Soon brightly colored shapes covered the walls of his studio—leaves, dancers, and abstract forms—with Matisse living among them.

In his final years, Matisse produced hundreds of cutout works. One of his monumental pieces from this period, *The Swimming Pool*, is a room-sized installation that surrounds the viewer with swimmers and sea creatures. Another, *Chapelle du Rosaire de Vence*, Matisse considered to be his masterpiece. Using the paper cutouts, Matisse designed the entire interior of a chapel including stained glass windows, murals, and wall hangings.

The cutouts became some of Matisse's most influential and recognizable works, blurring the lines between painting and sculpture. By embracing and adapting to his constraints, Matisse reinvented his own creative process and, in doing so, helped push the boundaries of art at that time.

More Constraints = More Creativity

Conventional wisdom about creativity tells us that freedom is your friend. A quote (often misattributed to Ralph Waldo Emerson) says, "Do not go where the path may lead, go instead where there is no path and leave a trail." George Clinton put it a bit more succinctly: "Free your mind and your ass will follow." And at some point, we've all heard "think outside the box."

The notion that creativity thrives in the absence of rules or constraints has inspired everything from retreats to motivational wall hangings to open-concept working spaces. It's everywhere. But where does this belief come from?

Interestingly, the "think outside the box" mantra does not come from the business world or even creativity research. It actually comes from something called the "nine-dots puzzle," which was developed by a chess master named Samuel Loyd. In the 1970s, psychologist J. P. Guilford adapted Loyd's puzzle for his research on problem-solving. Guilford's version of the puzzle is as follows: Look at the figure below. Without picking up your pencil, try to connect all the dots using only four straight lines. (Go ahead and try this puzzle for yourself.)

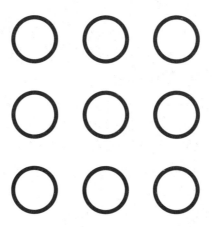

The trick to solving the nine-dots puzzle—as you may have figured out—is that you can extend the lines beyond the boundaries implied by the array of dots. And once you are aware of this trick, you realize that it is possible to solve the puzzle with only three lines, or even one line, depending on how far the lines extend. Hence the seductive thought that you can arrive at breakthrough ideas by setting aside the conventional assumptions that "box" your thinking in.

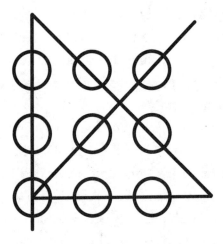

Guilford began using the nine-dots puzzle in his lectures, and the mantra quickly caught on. As psychologist Drew Boyd said, "Overnight, it seemed that creativity gurus everywhere were teaching managers how to think outside the box. Management consultants in the 1970s and 1980s even used this puzzle when making sales pitches to prospective clients. Because the solution is, in hindsight, deceptively simple, clients tended to admit they should have thought of it themselves. Because they hadn't, they were obviously not as creative or smart as they had previously thought and needed to call in creative experts."

Clearly, there is something about the "think outside the box" mantra that appeals to people. Perhaps it *feels* as though creativity ought to be wild and unfettered. But is it true in practice? Do people come up with better ideas when they have fewer rules or constraints?

In fact, research by psychologists Page Moreau and Darren Dahl shows exactly the opposite: People generate better ideas when they're given *more* constraints, not fewer.

In their studies, Moreau and Dahl asked college students to design children's toys. While this might sound like a dream assignment, there was a clever twist. The researchers gave participants a set of basic shapes to work with—things like handles, spheres, and pyramids. Some students were given complete freedom: They could use any shapes they wanted or none at all. Others faced increasingly strict rules, with the most constrained group having to incorporate exactly five specific shapes chosen by the researchers.

Think about the challenge this created. The "restricted" students couldn't just design any toy that popped into their heads—they had to figure out how to work with their assigned shapes, perhaps combining a pyramid with a handle in a way that made sense for a children's toy.

Once they finished, the designs were given to a panel of experts with significant experience in the toy industry. The experts rated each toy based on its market potential.

Whose toys do you think were rated most likely to succeed? According to the think-outside-the-box logic, the group with the most freedom should come up with the best toy designs. But that's not what happened. Instead, it was the participants who received the most constraints who came up with the best toy designs. When participants were given five randomly selected shapes and were told they had to use all of them, the resulting toy designs were rated by the experts as significantly more likely to succeed than the toys generated in the other conditions. More constraints resulted in better designs.

To figure out what explained this result, Moreau and Dahl examined the written logs that participants kept while they were coming up with their designs. And here's the golden nugget for us: The constraints led participants to approach the problem in a completely different way. Rather than defaulting to common toy ideas, participants began their ideation by thinking about the constraints: *Hmm . . . let's see. I have to use a cylinder, a pyramid, a handle, a cross, and a thin pole. What kind of a thing could I create that would use all five shapes?*

Approaching the problem in this way led to toy designs that were rated as more successful than those created by participants who were given complete freedom.

This result reinforces our previous discussions about the importance of problem finding (chapter 3) and having a specific, guiding question (chapter 4). In this case, the constraints led participants to engage in an entirely different kind of search. In the absence of constraints, participants searched broadly for "toy ideas," which led them to default to rather boring designs. But when there were constraints, participants searched much more narrowly for ideas that satisfied the criteria they had been given. Additionally, the researchers found that participants who were given more constraints spent significantly more time generating ideas. With a more specific guiding question in hand, those participants did more Digging and thus were more likely to unearth a truly creative idea.

Conceptual constraints like those used in the toy design study are not the only types of constraints that boost creativity. For example, research shows that in some situations, groups with smaller budgets come up with more creative (and better) solutions than groups with larger budgets. In this case, financial constraints limit the use of certain kinds of materials.

When Steven Spielberg made *Jaws*, the production quickly went over the modest studio budget of $4 million. The film was initially planned to heavily feature a mechanical shark. However, the three mechanical sharks on set—all nicknamed Bruce—frequently malfunctioned. This forced Spielberg to leave much to the audience's imagination, which, in the end, made those scenes with just the shark fin much more terrifying. There is a joke that the limited budget was also responsible for John Williams's classic *Jaws* theme consisting of only two notes, *bah-dum, bah-dum.*

How to Construct a Grid

This research tells us that rather than thinking outside the box, there is enormous value from thinking *inside* it. Constraints—the walls of the "box"—can spur new innovative solutions, help us formulate better and more interesting guiding questions, and, as we'll see next, facilitate the construction of grids, which is a tool for systematically searching for ideas and narrowing our focus.

Let's begin with a creative challenge. Here is one that I like to use with participants in my own research on creativity:

The Reality Show Challenge

Imagine you have been contacted by television producers, and they want your best idea for a brand-new reality show. The new show should be about a topic, or individuals, or a facet of life that hasn't been featured before—in other words, something new. And, of course, the producers are hoping that it will be a smash hit, so try to think of something that will really capture people's attention.

Take a few minutes to brainstorm new reality show ideas.

How did it go? Did you come up with anything good?

Now, let's try approaching this creative challenge using a grid. Much like an archeologist uses string to make their search organized, we will use grids to help you explore the conceptual space and consider topics that you might not have otherwise.

The grid that I'll use for this particular challenge, I call the What and Why Grid. There are, however, other kinds of grids and different forms they can take. At the end of this chapter, I've provided an example of another type of grid.

Step 1: Gather some data.

One way to start identifying constraints and relevant categories is to simply make a list of successful ideas in that topic area. Here are some of the most popular reality shows of the last several decades: *The Real World, Real Housewives, Big Brother, Survivor, Keeping Up with the Kardashians, The Bachelor, Queer Eye, Project Runway, RuPaul's Drag Race, Top Chef, Duck Dynasty, Deadliest Catch, Pawn Stars, 90 Day Fiancé, Shark Tank, Property Brothers, The Osbournes, American Chopper.*

Step 2: Generate categories for "what" and "why."

The What and Why Grid is based on the notion that the key aspects of a guiding question are basically the *what* (the type of idea/project) and the *why* (the value they your idea/project provides to people).

From our list of popular shows, we now want to create categories along these two dimensions:

- **What:** Based on our list, what are some different categories of reality shows?
- **Why:** Based on our list, what are some psychological benefits viewers get from watching a reality show (different types of entertainment, education, etc.)?

Here are the categories I came up with:

- **What:** Relationship Dynamics (*Kardashians, The Real World, Osbournes, The Bachelor, 90 Day Fiancé*), Competition (*Big Brother, Survivor, The Bachelor, Drag Race, Project Runway, Top*

Chef), Improvement (*Queer Eye, Property Brothers*), Business (*Duck Dynasty, Deadliest Catch, Pawn Stars, Shark Tank, American Chopper*).

Now, let's think about the benefits those shows may provide. Here are a few that jumped out to me:

- **Why**: Curiosity (a window into other people's lives), Inspiration (a sense of vicarious achievement or imagining oneself in the competition: "Hey, I could do that"), Variety (watching people whose lives are interesting and different).

Step 3: Construct a grid.

The next step is to construct a grid where the columns reflect the *what* and the rows reflect the *why*. These categories will provide the constraints to help you systematically search for promising topics.

What (your idea is)

A new reality television show focused on . . .

		Relationships	Competition	Improvement	Business
Why (the value that your idea provides)	Curiosity				
	Inspiration				
	Variety				

Step 4: Fill in the cells.

Next, we can fill in each of these cells. Some things to keep in mind as you do this: First—and I have said this multiple times already—there are huge benefits of doing what you know. So, as you're filling in the grid, you want to focus on topics or ideas that are within your area of expertise. Given that one area I am expert in is academics/higher education, I will try to come up with reality show ideas that are about this topic.

Second, stay flexible. If you're having trouble coming up with ideas for an entire row or column, feel free to drop it or replace it with something else. Again, there are no strict guidelines here, the goal is simply to get you thinking about the problem in a systematic way.

What (your idea is)

A new reality television show focused on . . .

		Relationships	Competition	Improvement	Business
Why (the value that your idea provides)	**Curiosity**	Professor Life: A look into lives of professors.	Top Grades: The dynamics between students as they compete for top grades in classes.	Grade Boost: Students receive mentoring from professors to improve their grades.	Administrators: Shows the behind-the-scenes dynamics of how universities run.
	Inspiration	Overcoming Odds: The triumphs of students from uncommon backgrounds.	Scholarship Race: Students compete in challenges for a scholarship prize.	Career Switch: Professionals return to university to pivot in their careers.	Innovators in Training: Follows students as they seek to turn their inventions into real businesses.
	Variety	Study Abroad: Follows students as they study abroad.	Major Makeover: Students undergo a series of experiences to find their true calling.	Getting Tenure: Follows the lives of faculty as they go up for tenure.	Dropouts: Follows students who drop out to pursue start-ups.

Step 5: Select the most promising idea and narrow in further.

Now we want to select a topic from this grid to explore further. As you can see, many of the ideas I generated are not good. But a few have promise. For example, I personally like the general idea of "Study Abroad," since there are a lot of different ways it could go: Who are the main characters—students, professors, locals? Are there multiple locations? Do the characters live together or separately? Is there a goal or challenge?

From here, the next step is to begin generating more concrete ideas (which we will focus on in detail in chapters 7 through 9). But when you take a step back and consider the relatively little amount of time and effort it takes to engage in this type of systematic thinking, you begin to see the immense power of this approach. In a short time, we generated several decent ideas—ideas that without a grid, I might not have ever considered. And by unpacking the cells in our grid further or using different criteria, I'm sure we could unlock many more.

For comparison, think back to the open-ended brainstorming that I asked you to engage in at the beginning of this section. My guess is that despite the lack of constraints, you probably came up with considerably fewer ideas, and those ideas were probably a lot less focused.

What if you construct a grid but don't like anything that you find? It's easy to simply begin again with a new set of categories. You can add additional categories or can drill down even deeper and continue to refine. The more time and effort you put into choosing the grid dimensions and thinking carefully about what goes into each of the cells, the better your results will be.

As one example of what this approach looks like in practice, consider the story of Charles and Ray Eames, the legendary designer couple who revolutionized the furniture industry.

In 1942, the Eameses received a rather strange request. It was World War II and the US government was facing significant challenges in treating battlefield injuries. Traditional metal splints used for broken or fractured limbs were proving inadequate—they were heavy, didn't conform to the body, and could exacerbate injuries when wounded soldiers were transported. At the time, the Eameses had already begun experimenting with molded plywood to create sculptural objects. They had developed a method for molding plywood into complex shapes using heat and pressure. This work caught the attention of the military, who saw the potential of plywood for medical applications: It was lightweight, could cheaply be mass-produced, and could be molded to conform to the human body.

The Eameses were awarded a contract to produce plywood splints for the military. But then the couple realized that if plywood could be molded to fit people's legs, it could also be molded to fit people's backsides—hence, furniture. This realization gave rise to a period of intense experimentation. Suddenly, the Eames workshop resembled a laboratory, where they systematically tested different techniques to bend and mold plywood into different shapes and different chair configurations. They produced countless prototypes and failures. In testing each combination of elements and eliminating what did not work, their focus became increasingly concentrated on only the most promising directions.

Ultimately, their exploration paid off. The molded plywood furniture designs that emerged from this period—like the LCW (Lounge Chair Wood) and the DCW (Dining Chair Wood)—became instant classics. Not only have their designs been hugely influential, but their investigations also paved the way for using plywood to make furniture, which is now a standard in the industry.

The Unconscious Grid

Grids work because the constraints of a creative challenge help us narrow in and consider options that we might not have thought of otherwise. But part of their effectiveness, I believe, stems from the fact that they are reflecting something much deeper about how our minds naturally want to engage in the creative process. Our brains thrive on structure and organization and the ability to predict what's next—so, there are many instances in which we will default into a "grid way of thinking" even when we are not consciously aware of it.

To understand what I mean by this, let's consider an example from the world of fiction writing. If you read interviews with many best-selling novelists, they tend to say the same thing: Great stories write themselves. Many authors report the phenomenon of characters "hijacking" a story and taking control of the plot. For example, Jon Fosse, recipient of the 2023 Nobel Prize, said of his process, "When I'm writing well, I have this very clear and distinct feeling that what I'm writing on is already written. It's somewhere out there. I just have to write it down before it disappears."

George Saunders describes, "There is something wonderful in watching a figure emerge from the stone unsummoned, feeling the presence of something within you, the writer, and also beyond you—something consistent, willful, and benevolent, that seems to have a plan, which seems to be: to lead you to your own higher ground."

Or, in a *Writer's Digest* article titled "Sometimes the Story Writes Itself," the author Cheryl A. Ossola suggests writers need to get out of the story's way. In writing *The Wild Impossibility*, Ossola says, "Other characters are downright pushy. Designated as walk-ons, suddenly they're clamoring for supporting roles."

So, what's going on here? What does it mean for a story to "write itself," or for characters to write their own plot? Are these authors possessed? Is this BS, or is there something deeper at work?

To understand what I think may be occurring in these situations, consider fascinating research by cognitive scientists Deena Weisberg and my friend and collaborator Paul Bloom. Their research demonstrated that children as young as three years old recognize there is an "intuitive cosmology" to fictional realms. In other words, what happens in one fictional universe does not (and cannot) affect what happens in a different fictional universe.

For example, Superman has a host of superhuman abilities: He can fly, lift a train, has X-ray vision, and more. But any three-year-old will tell you that the one thing Superman can't do is visit SpongeBob in the underwater city of Bikini Bottom. The worlds are completely separate. The universe of Superman, Lex Luthor, and Lois Lane does not contain Bikini Bottom. Conversely, the universe of SpongeBob with Patrick Star and Squidward does not contain any inkling of Metropolis or kryptonite. It wouldn't make sense.

But, importantly, no one has to teach us this fact—as a parent, it's mind-boggling to think of how you might even try. Rather, it is a constraint, a structure, that we intuitively grasp about the genre of fiction itself—fictional universes are distinct; whatever deviations there are from reality in one realm do not spill over into others.

A related idea, proposed by the philosopher David Lewis, is the notion of "truth in fiction." Lewis argues that every possible world, including fictional ones, has its own set of truths. Whereas fictional worlds often deviate from the actual world, those deviations, according to Lewis, cannot be so extreme that they render the fictional world completely unrecognizable. There is a delicate balance to be maintained. Even in fiction, we expect that some things might be different enough to be interesting, but not so different that the world itself becomes entirely incomprehensible.

Weisberg and Bloom, along with others, have suggested that these implicit rules—that you can't alter too much, or that different fictional realms cannot interact—provide important constraints on how we invent fictional worlds. When we, as an author, imagine fictional worlds, our default is to assume the world is identical to ours. We then begin to modify this world by changing one or two elements at a time. For example, if you begin to write about a fictional world where the characters can time travel, you will likely assume that all other aspects of the world are held constant—for instance, that there is gravity or that people need oxygen to survive. After the world is established, events unfold, but the plotline and events must adhere to these original rules. You can think of this as a version of Gridding, where different elements of this fictional world constrain what is possible.

There are also grids for the events that can take place in that fictional world and grids for the psychologies of different characters. As an author goes deeper and deeper into a story, the grids for that fictional world, the events therein, and the psychology of the characters all begin to interact.

And here's the important part: For the story to make sense, there are a finite number of ways things can go—a finite number of plausible interactions that still adhere to all the constraints that are in place.

I imagine then that part of what is going on when authors report that "the story writes itself" is that, subconsciously, the author has in mind all the constraints of the fictional world and the characters within it. As these grids become more detailed and complex, the interaction of these different constraints becomes increasingly deterministic. As the author's unconscious mind then tests various possibilities that satisfy the constraints, some combinations "click."

These outcomes bubble up into conscious awareness, giving rise to the feeling that the character—and not the author—is in the driver's seat.

What does this mean for creativity more broadly? The key takeaway is that constraints are tools. They guide your process, shaping the options you consider and making certain paths feel natural or "right." By understanding and leveraging these constraints, you can tap into that flow where the work seems to create itself. The key is to explore the possibilities within your framework systematically, making creativity less about waiting for a spark and more about navigating the structure you've built. The clearer your constraints, the more effortlessly creativity unfolds.

Constraints Are Creativity's Engine

Constraints are not the enemies of creativity—they are its catalysts. When you take the time to identify the constraints of your creative challenge, you're creating a framework that guides your search toward outcomes that might otherwise remain hidden. And by organizing these constraints using a structured framework like a grid, you can often generate many more ideas than you would have otherwise. Whether it's product design, artistic pursuits, or writing, the principle holds: The more clearly you define your boundaries—the walls of your box—the more effectively you can think within them and the more likely you are to uncover something great.

Exercises

Gridding is a powerful tool, allowing you to refine your creative direction and systematically explore a conceptual space. Below, I've included another type of grid as well as an exercise to encourage thinking about how constraints can be turned into opportunities.

Exercise 16: One-Dimensional Grid

Another way to approach Gridding is to think of potential options along a single dimension. For example, suppose you have a small business selling spices and you're interested in developing a new product. How can Gridding help?

- **Begin by considering some of the relevant categories:** Is the spice a single ingredient or a blend? If it's a blend, does it have an intended purpose—e.g., a certain type of cuisine? Is it intended to be used for a certain type of meal or at a certain time of day? What is the context? What is the delivery mechanism?
- **Construct the grid.** For each of these categories, list all the options you can think of. Here is a table that I came up with, though I'm sure there are many more categories and options.
- **Locate existing ideas.** What exists already? Begin crossing out options. If you need to, make multiple copies of your grid.
- **Look for open space.** Now begin to look for opportunities (i.e., gaps in the grid). Are there combinations of options that don't exist already but seem promising? For example, when I completed this table, I was intrigued by the lack of single-use spice-blend packs for use on the go. Why not create single-use packets of spice blends that emulate the spice profiles of a particular cuisine that are easy to pack and travel with?

Ingredients	Intended Foods	Meal	Context	Delivery Mechanism/ Size
Salt	Poultry	Breakfast	At Home	Typical Retail Size
Black Pepper	Beef	Brunch	Restaurants	Bulk
Garlic Powder	Pork	Lunch	Outdoors	Single Use
Onion Powder	Lamb	Dinner	Camping	Pocket-Sized
Cinnamon	Seafood	Snack	BBQ	Grinder Bottles
Cumin	Vegetables	Dessert	At Work	Refill Packs
Turmeric	Legumes	Beverage	Celebrations	Subscription Boxes
Chili Powder	Grains	Kids' Meals	Festivals	Gift Sets (Themed)
Paprika	Soups and Stews		On the Go	Combo Packs (for Recipes)
Nutmeg	Baked Goods		Leftovers	Specialty Containers
Coriander	Sauces and Dips			Artisanal
Cardamom	Eggs			
Cloves	Pasta and Noodles			
Fennel Seed	Salads			
Mustard Seed	Snacks			
Saffron	Drinks			
Ginger	Cocktails			
Cayenne Pepper				
Star Anise				
Allspice				

Exercise 17: Constraints into Opportunities

The goal of this exercise is to practice turning constraints into opportunities.

- **List out all known constraints** (e.g., budget, time, materials).

- **Imagine one specific person** who you would love to engage with your idea—it could be a customer, a viewer, a listener, or reader. Make them "real." Give them a name, a personal history, and goals. Most important, define what they seek to gain from engaging with your work.

- **For each constraint, think of ways you could turn this limitation into an advantage** or opportunity for this person. This could involve using the constraint to simplify the project, serve a different need, or target a different audience. (For example, if your budget is limited, perhaps you can focus on creating a minimalist design that resonates with a design-minded person.)

- **Consider how other audiences might view these constraints.** Imagine a different potential audience member, with a different name, different characteristics, and different goals. Would any of these constraints particularly benefit them?

6.

Transplanting

Charles Darrow was down on his luck, unemployed and struggling. Then, in a moment of genius, he invented the game of Monopoly. He sold the game to Parker Brothers, became a millionaire, and the rest is history. Inspiration and inventiveness saved the day.

The one catch? The story isn't true.

In fact, Monopoly has an entirely different origin. Those who delight in the game's windfalls or scorn the inevitable feuds it incites do not have Darrow to thank but instead a progressive polymath named Elizabeth "Lizzie" Magie.

Born in Macomb, Illinois, in 1866, Magie was a woman of diverse talents and interests. She was an inventor, writer, feminist, and progressive thinker. Unusual for her day, Magie did not marry until she was in her mid-forties. In her spare time, she wrote poetry and performed comedy. Her father, James Magie, was a newspaper publisher and abolitionist, and that early exposure to politics fueled Magie's desire to address the social injustices of her day, particularly those stemming from wealth inequality.

In 1904, Magie received a patent for The Landlord's Game, a game she developed as a demonstration of the land value tax proposed by economist Henry George. George's philosophy argued that individuals should own the value they produce themselves, but that the economic value derived from natural resources, including land, should be shared equally among members of society. Magie's game was intended to educate players about the benefits of George's proposal.

The board of The Landlord's Game was a square with properties laid out around the perimeter that players could buy, sell, and rent. Taxes were also parts of the game, serving as mechanisms to redistribute wealth and illustrate the effects of George's theories. The game featured two sets of rules: the "Prosperity" rule, under which all players benefited from wealth created by the development of land, and the "Monopolist" rule, where the goal was to create monopolies and crush opponents, reflecting the negative aspects of capitalism.

Unfortunately, The Landlord's Game did not have the widespread influence Magie had hoped. The game was manufactured in limited quantities, and it wasn't until nearly three decades later that the game became popular.

During the Great Depression, Charles Darrow became familiar with The Landlord's Game and presented it to Parker Brothers, who convinced Magie to sell her patent to them for only $500. The Prosperity rules were removed, such that only Monopolist rules remained, and the game was fittingly called Monopoly. The result was the best-selling board game of all time.

Although Magie did not receive the credit she deserved for Monopoly, the success of the game she created highlights an important principle of creative discovery: *transplanting*.

Transplanting is the process of taking existing concepts from one domain and applying them somewhere new and unexpected. Magie did this when she took academic ideas from economics and used them to develop an engaging board game. And in this chapter, we'll see how creatives of all types have used the principle of transplanting to unearth new technologies, new forms of art, and more.

Transplanting works because there are often deeper veins of commonality that run across seemingly different domains. As a result, a concept from one area can reveal unexpected opportunities when it is applied elsewhere. Charles Babbage demonstrated this when he realized that the punch cards used to create textile patterns for looms could also store mathematical operations, paving the way for computers. Or the artist James Turrell, who has used principles from perceptual psychology to develop groundbreaking works in which he appears to sculpt and paint with light.

In a rather literal version of transplanting, artist Tim Klein has found inspiration by realizing that many puzzle manufacturers reuse the same die-cut pattern. Klein discovered that he could swap out pieces from completely different puzzles, combining them to make bizarre, fantastical images. Klein told me this about his process:

I often feel not so much like an artist as an archaeologist, reconstructing a shattered picture that has been lying latent for decades, waiting for me to come along and discover it. I find it fascinating that the elements of this surreal image have been there all along, hiding in plain sight in dusty old puzzle boxes stacked together on someone's game room shelf, unknown to anyone until I came along and pieced it together. It makes me wonder how many other such fragmented potential montages exist out there amongst the world's millions of jigsaw puzzles, never to be "discovered" by anyone—and how many of them may be even more striking than the ones I've managed to discover so far?

Who Holds the Cage Holds the Bird by artist Tim Klein.

When we look at one set of ideas through the lens of something completely different, we can uncover possibilities that were there all along, waiting to be discovered. The trick is learning to recognize these underlying patterns—the "die-cut shapes"—and make meaningful connections across them.

The Three R's of Transplanting: Recognition, Relevance, and Refinement

How do we take different topics and merge them into something new and meaningful? The process of transplanting can be broken down into three stages: recognition, relevance, and refinement. First, we need to identify opportunities for connection. Next, we must understand how elements align (or don't) between the two areas. Finally, we refine how these elements come together, fine-tuning until we discover something that works in the new context.

Stage 1: Recognition

Transplanting begins with spotting connections across different areas. Sometimes this happens by accident. The cooking potential of the magnetron was realized only when it melted the candy bar in Percy Spencer's pocket, leading to the development of the microwave oven. Rogaine was initially developed to treat high blood pressure until researchers discovered that, over time, it could help combat hair loss. Interestingly, Viagra was also originally a hypertension drug until researchers discovered that it had a different, more conspicuous side effect.

But more often recognition comes from careful observation, noticing how solutions in one area might address creative challenges in another. When the Japanese high-speed train the Shinkansen was first constructed, engineers realized they had a problem: The train traveled so fast that when it exited tunnels, it created a sonic-boom effect. The noise was clearly an issue for people living near the tracks.

The solution came from an unexpected source. Eiji Nakatsu, an engineer working on the Shinkansen, was an avid bird-watcher. With his knowledge of many bird species, he recalled the silent, streamlined dive of the kingfisher bird. It turns out that the kingfisher's beak is particularly well adapted for minimizing resistance as it enters the water so as not to alert its prey. This observation led Nakatsu to redesign the train's nose, which mimicked the shape of the kingfisher's beak. The new design fixed the sonic-boom problem. It also reduced air resistance, allowing the train to run at a stunning 200 miles per hour while using significantly less energy.

There is also the example of Janet Stephens, a professional hairstylist, who recognized the application of her expertise to historical studies. One day, on a visit to the Walters Art Museum in Baltimore, Stephens found herself transfixed by a Roman bust. She was struck by the intricate hairstyle of the sculpture. Could she reproduce the same configurations with people's natural hair? At the time, most historians regarded the hairstyles depicted in ancient Roman art as too complex to have been actual hair.

Stephens then set out on a multiyear project to re-create the hairstyles of ancient Romans and Greeks using only the tools that would have been available thousands of years ago. Her research was self-directed, drawing from a blend of historical texts and her years of accumulated hairstyling expertise. She practiced endlessly on volunteer models. Eventually, her research paid off. Through careful experimentation, she discovered that ancient women used needle and thread to literally stitch their hair together. Her discovery provided an important window into the social and cultural practices of the times, and she even went on to publish her findings in an academic journal.

Stage 2: Relevance

The second stage of transplanting—relevance—involves identifying the precise overlaps between domains. During this critical phase, we strip down each set of ideas to find specific connections between elements— like seeing how a kingfisher's streamlined beak could inform the shape of a train's nose. These mappings help us understand exactly how concepts from one domain can be meaningfully applied to another.

The term for this process in cognitive science is *analogical reasoning*. When we use analogies, familiarity with a concrete example helps us understand relationships that are otherwise abstract and difficult to grasp. But analogies are more than just clever comparisons. A good analogy helps us see relationships we might not have considered before, understand cause and effect, and perhaps even make new predictions about the future. The cognitive scientist Douglas Hofstadter went so far as to call analogies "the engine of cognition" (which, of course, is also analogy).

As one demonstration of the power of analogies, consider a classic dilemma presented by psychologists Mary Glick and Keith Holyoak:

Suppose you are a doctor faced with a patient who has a tumor in his stomach. Unless the tumor is destroyed, the patient will die. There is a kind of ray that can be used to destroy the tumor, but there is a catch: If the rays reach the tumor all at once at a sufficiently high intensity, the tumor will be destroyed. But unfortunately, at this intensity, the healthy tissue that the rays pass through on the way to the tumor will also be destroyed. At lower intensities, the rays are harmless to healthy tissue, but they will not affect the tumor either. What type of procedure might be used to destroy the tumor with the rays while at the same time avoid destroying healthy tissue?

When Glick and Holyoak asked participants to solve this problem, most were stumped.

However, for another group of participants, the psychologists first preceded the problem with a fictional story:

A general wanted to attack a fortress. There were several roads that led to the fortress from different sides, but each road had mines. Individual soldiers could pass through the mines, but if the entire army went together, the mines would detonate. To solve the problem the general divided the army into smaller groups and sent each party along a different road. The smaller groups converged on the fortress at the same time and were successful at taking the fortress.

For the participants who read the fictional story first, nearly all of them correctly solved the medical puzzle: If the doctors could somehow disperse the ray from different angles, converging on the tumor at the same time, they could destroy the tumor while sparing the tissue. With the story preceding it, the answer now seems obvious.

But when you think about what is actually occurring in your mind, it is quite complex. Essentially, you are having to map different elements of the story that, on the surface, have nothing to do with one another—the connection between the fortress and tumor, the army and the rays, mines and tissue damage, and so on. It's not until you link up all these different elements that you realize the solution in the story is a good solution for the medical puzzle. And yet this is something your brain naturally wants to do—in fact, it is something that the human mind does incredibly well.

Think of this very book, combining archeological digs and the creative process. This analogy occurred to me after years of researching creativity. The more I researched and understood, the more I became convinced that creativity is not a process of simply conjuring ideas out of thin air. Rather, I started to see it as something that more closely resembles a process of discovery.

Then one day, I was listening to one of my favorite bands, the Pixies, and something clicked. In their song "Dig for Fire," the lyrics hit me. I made a connection to creativity and the discovery of ideas more generally. I thought of archeology. As I began to learn more about archeology, relevance came into focus. I began to see connections across the two domains—for example, in the stages of Surveying, Gridding, Digging, and Sifting.

Suddenly, it wasn't just a cute comparison. The analogy was propelling me forward and leading me down new paths that I never would have considered before. A new creative idea emerged that I would go on to test and refine.

Stage 3: Refinement

In the final stage of transplanting, promising connections across domains must be put into practice. As in engineering, success comes from building and refining prototypes until you discover what works. Each iteration reveals new challenges and opportunities.

One wonderful illustration of this comes from the story of Karen Wynn Fonstad, a geographer who used transplanting to create something entirely new in the world of fantasy literature. Fonstad's creative journey began with a cold call to J. R. R. Tolkien's publisher. As a devoted fan of *The Lord of the Rings* books (she had read them more than thirty times), Fonstad pitched the idea of creating the first scientific atlas of Tolkien's imaginary world. To her surprise, she got an immediate yes.

But that quick yes led to the real challenge: figuring out how to actually do it. For the next two and a half years, Fonstad worked nonstop. As a professor and mother, the only spare time she found to work on the project was late at night while her children slept. She made multiple trips to Marquette University to study Tolkien's original manuscripts, indexing every geographical reference and wrestling with how to adapt real-world cartographic principles to a fictional realm, like mapping the morphology of the Shire and analyzing the plate tectonics that might have shaped Mordor.

In 1981, her atlas, with its 172 hand-drawn maps, was published, transforming how people thought about fictional worlds. Readers felt like they could physically explore a realm that had existed only in their imaginations. As one fantasy author put it, Fonstad's work was "the Velvet Underground of fantasy mapmaking—everyone who read it went out and got graph paper and mapped something."

While Fonstad successfully transplanted geography to fiction by drawing primarily on her own expertise, sometimes successful refinement requires a more collaborative approach—like the story of Gabriella Papadakis and Guillaume Cizeron, a figure skating pair who changed the sport by transplanting principles from modern dance.

The French couple began skating together when they were only ten years old, and as they developed, they became interested in pushing the boundaries of traditional figure skating. Modern dance offered the potential to explore new conceptual terrain. But translating modern dance to figure skating posed some real physical challenges. Skaters are zipping around on rock-hard ice, traveling at speeds upward of 15 miles per hour, balanced precariously on, essentially, a pair of steak knives. Modern dance, in contrast, embraces off-balance positions, sudden direction changes, and body positions that clash with the basic rules of skating. The gap between these art forms seemed impossible to bridge.

It didn't really click until Papadakis and Cizeron began collaborating with modern dance experts like Samuel Chouinard and Axelle

Munezero. For instance, in preparation for the 2022 Olympics, the skaters decided to incorporate "waacking," a distinctive dance style that emerged from underground LGBTQ bars in Los Angeles. Waacking is characterized by rapid and sharp, rhythmic arm movements that are unusual in figure skating. But with the help of Munezero, one of the originators of the style, the program they developed went on to set an Olympic record.

Whether mapping an imaginary world or translating modern dance to ice, successful refinement demands technical mastery and persistence. The task often requires multiple iterations and the insight of other experts.

Successful Transplanting Depends on Brokers

These "other experts" play such a crucial role in transplanting that they deserve special attention. In fact, there's actually a name for these crucial connectors: *brokers.*

Ronald Burt, a pioneer of social network theory, developed this idea of brokers: individuals who connect different parts of a social network. They bridge gaps in information or knowledge, what Burt calls "structural holes." By linking different clusters of people, brokers enable information and ideas to flow across people who might not normally interact. Their access to diverse perspectives puts them in a unique position to spot and combine ideas in new ways.

In the figure skating example, modern dance experts like Chouinard and Munezero helped bridge the gap between dance and skating. But successful transplanting often needs different kinds of brokers at different stages; for example, someone to help spot initial connections, someone to link key elements together, and someone to help with refinement.

A lovely illustration of this idea at work can be seen in the development of the carbon dating method, which is the story of transplanting ideas from chemistry to archeology.

In the 1940s, Willard Libby, a chemistry professor at the University of Chicago, realized that radioactive isotopes could be used to date organic materials. Since carbon-14 decays at a known rate (a half-life of 5,730 years), Libby reasoned that by measuring the remaining carbon-14 in an ancient sample, he could reveal its age with remarkable precision.

A key connection, however, came through Libby's undergraduate research assistant, a young man named James Arnold. While home for Christmas break, Arnold mentioned the new method to his father, who happened to be an amateur archaeologist. His father immediately recognized its potential and called his friend at the Metropolitan Museum of Art, who sent Arnold and his father a box of archaeological samples. When Arnold returned to campus after the break, he brought the samples with him, giving Libby his first opportunity to test his method on real historical artifacts.

But Libby knew he needed another set of experts: archaeologists who could validate that his method was historically accurate. After analyzing the samples, Libby presented his findings at a lunchtime lecture to his colleagues in the archaeology department. The archaeologists immediately saw the method's potential and contacted the American Anthropological Association. And in turn, the association formed a committee, who assembled teams of archaeologists, geologists, and chemists to perfect the method. After several years of careful refinement, the carbon dating method was ready. In short order, carbon dating revolutionized the field of archeology, Libby was awarded a Nobel Prize in Chemistry, and new applications were soon being explored in climate science, forensics, and beyond.

This story illustrates how different types of brokers can shape each stage of transplanting. James Arnold, Libby's undergraduate research assistant, was pivotal in forging an important initial connection between chemists and archeologists (recognition). The archaeology faculty who attended Libby's talk were important for linking his method to existing dating techniques (relevance). Finally, the association's committee formalized collaborations between archaeologists and chemists to refine the method. Without these brokers working at multiple stages, the idea might have remained just an interesting theory. For transplanting to be successful, it needed multiple brokers, working at multiple stages.

Transplanting Can Awaken Sleeping Beauties

In 2015, researchers at Indiana University discovered a fascinating effect they called "sleeping beauties." While most ideas in science and technology reach their peak influence shortly after they're published, the researchers found that some ideas can lie dormant for decades or even centuries before they awake, suddenly exploding into prominence.

Take the Möbius strip, a curious geometric form defined as a surface with only one side and one edge; you can make one yourself by giving a thin paper strip a half-twist before joining its ends. Two mathematicians, August Ferdinand Möbius and Johann Benedict Listing, independently discovered the Möbius strip in 1858 (another case of multiple discovery). But despite its elegant form, the idea of Möbius strip lay dormant for one hundred years.

Then in the 1950s, it awoke from its slumber. All of a sudden, the Möbius strip was being used everywhere—in conveyor belts, recording tapes, typewriter ribbons, computer printer cartridges, and electronics.

The researchers naturally wondered, what wakes up these sleeping beauty ideas? They found that the answer came down to transplanting. In the vast majority of cases, the sleeping beauties awoke when they were applied in an entirely new domain. Someone from a different field or industry had spotted how the idea could be used to solve a totally different creative problem.

The sleeping beauty phenomenon reinforces the core thesis of this book: Many breakthrough ideas exist already, just in unexpected places. Elizabeth Magie's game, Nakatsu's train, the figure skating of Papadakis and Cizeron, Fonstad's mapping of Middle-earth. These stories show that creative breakthroughs do not come from inventing something new but from discovering existing ideas and realizing their potential in new contexts.

The challenge is creating conditions where transplanting can flourish. For organizations, this might mean creating thoughtful physical spaces that foster chance interactions or more deliberate mixers like rotations and residencies. But individuals can cultivate these conditions too through research, conversations across disciplines, or simply remaining open to unexpected influences. Janet Stephens wasn't part of any formal research institution when she made her breakthrough about Roman hairstyles. She simply followed her curiosity where it led.

The key is developing a state of mind that celebrates this kind of openness to discovery. The most innovative thinkers recognize that expertise in one domain can illuminate insights in another, and they remain alert to the applications that others might overlook. Often the most profound ideas come from recognizing that an elegant solution is out there already. We just needed the right lens to see it.

Exercises

The following exercises are designed to explore transplanting, focusing on "the 3R's" of the process: recognition, relationships, and refinement.

Exercise 18: Fresh Perspective

The goal of this exercise is to foster the notion of transplanting by applying insights from a totally different domain.

- **Pick a current creative challenge**—a project you're working on or a creative problem you are stuck on.

- **Switch lenses.** Choose a simple activity or hobby that you regularly engage in has nothing to do with your challenge (e.g., baking, gardening, or playing chess).

- **Spend several minutes thinking** about how the tools, mindset, or skills from that other activity might relate to your problem. For example, how is my creative challenge like baking? What tools from gardening may help me with this problem?

- **Write down one possible application.** Even if it's silly or impractical, note one way this new perspective might change how you approach your current challenge.

- **If you hit a dead end,** simply pick a different activity.

Exercise 19: The Transplantation Game

This is a game designed to engage transplanting by merging concepts from diverse fields. Note, this game requires two or more people.

Preparation:

- **Schedule a session** with a friend or colleague who has expertise in a different field or industry. This game works best when participants have distinctly different areas of expertise, maximizing the potential for diverse and unexpected idea combinations.

- **Create Idea Decks.** Each participant prepares a deck of cards, with each card representing a unique idea, concept, topic, or problem from their field of expertise. Aim for a deck of at least five cards.

- **Decorate or design** the cards if you wish.

Playing the Game:

- **Each player shuffles their deck of idea cards.** Simultaneously, both players draw one card from the top of their decks and place the card face up on the table.

- **Take a moment to explain your card to your partner**, providing a brief overview of the concept, its significance, and any relevant context. This ensures both players have a foundational understanding before attempting to combine ideas.

- **Generate Connections.** Set a timer for five minutes dedicated to discussing how the two drawn ideas could be combined into something new—a new product, service, artwork, or concept. Consider how elements from each idea can complement or enhance the other.

- **No idea is too far-fetched at this stage.** The goal is to generate as many potential connections as possible.

GRIDDING: THE BIG TAKEAWAYS

The main idea in Gridding is to make your search more targeted and organized. Tools at your disposal include a guiding question, understanding the relevant constraints, a systematic framework (i.e., a grid), and transplanting.

What to keep in mind:

- **Develop a guiding question.** Think of this as your compass. Clearly define your "what" and "why." Your guiding question is a work in progress. As you continue to brainstorm, research, and get feedback, refine your guiding question to make it more precise.

- **Use a grid.** Allow the constraints of the problem to dictate the structure of your search space. Constraints are not the enemy of creativity; they are the engine. Use the grid to identify promising areas to explore. From there, narrow in further for more focused brainstorming.

- **Harness the power of transplanting.** Many great ideas have come from making cross-disciplinary connections and applying what is already known in totally new ways.

PART III

Digging

It's like being a safe breaker. You're listening for the right
click, painting and painting and painting
until the right thing happens.

—ELIZABETH MURRAY, ARTIST

T his section is about Digging: the process of generating ideas, testing out variations, and unearthing the early fragments of something that might become great.

Once you have a guiding question and a promising place to explore, the job is simple . . . in theory: Get as much out of the ground as you can. In practice, though, this is where people start to get in their own way. Even when we *know* we're supposed to generate a lot of ideas, we flinch. We second-guess. We fall in love with the first decent idea and stop too soon. We dig a single hole and walk away thinking we've seen the whole site.

This section is about how to avoid that. It's about how to keep searching for long enough that something truly interesting emerges.

You're not looking for the one right idea. You're looking for a set of ideas—a portfolio of possibilities—that you can test, reshape, and refine. That means working past the obvious answers, experimenting broadly, and staying open to surprise. It also means learning to override some very persistent biases, like the belief that creativity fades with age (it doesn't) or that good ideas come only from certain people (they don't). Many of us tune out or sideline our most valuable collaborators without realizing it. We ignore chance encounters, underestimate the importance of social acquaintances, and retreat inward just when our collaborations matter most.

We'll also talk about something harder to define but just as important: the spark. If you dig long enough, you may hit on something that catches fire. That spark starts pulling other elements into its orbit, and suddenly everything starts clicking into place. These are ideas that are worth waiting for. And when you find one, you realize something that sounds almost backward: The more time you spend searching, the *less* work you'll need to do from there.

This section is about everything that makes the brainstorming process succeed or fail: structure, volume, collaboration, randomness, and the spark that sets your process ablaze.

7.

More Is More

If there's one principle—one secret—that reliably improves creative success, it's this: *Generate more ideas.* Dig more holes. Go longer than feels reasonable. Then keep going.

It's what the data show across nearly every creative discipline. The most successful artists, composers, inventors, scientists, and entrepreneurs have one thing in common: They're prolific. And that doesn't mean that all their ideas make it out into the world. Most don't. Johann Sebastian Bach composed over a thousand pieces, many of which are rarely performed. Thomas Edison held more than a thousand patents, including duds like cement furniture, a creepy talking doll, and the electric pen (which later inspired modern tattoo needles). James Dyson developed over five thousand prototypes before ultimately settling on the design for the bagless vacuum. Innovators like Benjamin Franklin, George Washington Carver, Margaret Knight, and Beulah Louise Henry were serial experimenters whose greatest ideas emerged only after hundreds of others didn't.

When we look at the stars in any creative field, there's usually a wide gap between what we see and what actually happened. We see a polished final product. But behind that work is something far messier. Trial after trial, false starts, and wrong turns. That *is* the process. You rarely find a great idea by aiming directly at it. You find it by generating enough raw material for the right idea to emerge.

I'm certainly not the first person to recognize this fact. Linus Pauling, the two-time Nobel Laureate, famously said, "The best way to have a good idea is to have a lot of ideas." The question is, Do people actually follow this advice? Do people search long enough before calling it quits?

In a fascinating series of studies, researchers Brian Lucas and Loran Nordgren asked individuals to engage in a brainstorming task, such as coming up with ideas for how a charity could increase donations. Before the participants began brainstorming, Lucas and Nordgren first asked each to predict how productive they expected their idea generation would be over a five-minute period: How productive during the first minute? During the second minute? During the third minute? And so on.

Reliably, people expected the first two minutes to be productive and then a sharp drop-off after that: a bake sale, a raffle, door-to-door solicitations. Really, how many ideas for fundraisers could there be?

Then participants completed the brainstorming task. Interestingly, the researchers observed that the first minute was strong, as was the second minute. But then, instead of taking a nosedive, participants just kept on generating more ideas. The third minute was even more productive than the second, the fourth more productive than that. The researchers conducted this experiment eight times with different groups of participants, and in nearly every case, the final minute of brainstorming was drastically more productive than the first—quite contrary to people's expectations.

What's more, when Lucas and Nordgren had a different group of participants rate the quality of the ideas, raters scored the ideas generated during the latter half of the sessions as more promising than the ideas generated during the first half.

The researchers dubbed this phenomenon the *creative cliff illusion*. After an initial bout of brainstorming, most people thought that they would "fall off the cliff" and any additional time was unlikely to pay off. Yet when people are forced to keep going, they come up with many more and better ideas than they anticipated. Similar results were observed over much longer durations. For example, when creative professionals were asked to work on a real-life creative problem over the course of five days.

One takeaway from this research is that in generating ideas we should "dig lots of holes"—and importantly, many more than you think. Keep searching for ideas, especially after the first impulse to give up kicks in. A good rule of thumb is that just when you think you've exhausted every idea you can come up with, that's probably when your process is really heating up. That's the point at which you

The Creative Cliff Illusion

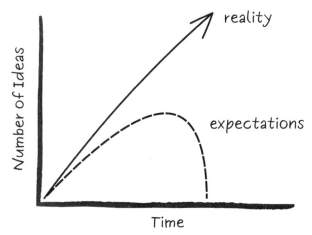

should redouble your efforts and continue generating ideas for a second round and a third after that.

This applies broadly: If you're trying to name your product or small business, aim to generate one hundred or even five hundred names. If you're tackling a business challenge, don't limit yourself to a single brainstorming session. Instead, schedule multiple focused sessions over several days. If you're planning a fundraiser for your community, fill up an entire stack of Post-it Notes with ideas. The reality is that most people underinvest in the ideation phase, often rushing to implement the first workable solution they find. It's hard to overstate the benefits of simply generating as many ideas as possible.

Think of it like an archaeological dig. What if the team packed up their equipment the moment they had their first find? That initial discovery might be just the beginning of a much larger find lying beneath the surface.

When we abandon the search too early, many other promising ideas will go unnoticed. As a result, we wind up settling. We find ourselves selecting among a pool of ideas that are ultimately less innovative and less valuable than those we might have discovered if we'd continued a bit longer.

Pushing Past the Creative Cliff

Why do we stop Digging for ideas early? One explanation is related to how we retrieve memories. We have two memory systems: long-term memory and working memory. Long-term memory is our vast store of knowledge, personal events, and semantic meaning. It is everything you know and the events from your life. It is the library.

Working memory, by contrast, is the stuff that is top of mind here and now. It is the so-called theater of the mind. You can think of it as your desk within the library.

In an actual library, all the resources aren't immediately available to you. To reference something, you first need to retrieve it and bring it to your desk before you can look at it. Similarly with memory, not all of your knowledge is immediately available. You need to first retrieve the information from your long-term memory and bring it into working memory before you can access and use it.

Here's why this distinction is important: When you are asked to generate ideas, such as ideas for a fundraiser, you will go to your long-term library and start grabbing the ideas that are related. And more likely than not, you will make the associations that are easiest to retrieve. Your brain is not lazy, but like all things in nature, it doesn't like to do more work than it needs to.

So now you've grabbed a handful of mental references and I ask you, "How long will it take you to find a good idea?" You look down on your "desk," see the modest stack, and say, "Two minutes, maybe three." And sure enough, if I ask you to start generating ideas, you will start essentially combing through what's on your desk and listing off ideas.

What's the problem? The problem is that you know way more than this. The references you grabbed aren't all your ideas on the topic. Not even close. They were just the first ones you selected. Moreover, they were probably the most boring, obvious, well-associated references. To get to the good stuff, you need to start really Digging around in the depths of your long-term memory.

As we discussed in chapter 4, you'll need an interesting guiding question to encourage deeper search. And as you follow this guiding question, new lines of thinking will open up, which will unlock more ideas, and so on.

Whenever I think of this idea, I recall my time as a graduate student mining the "stacks" at Yale's Sterling Library to recover journal articles. The space was so expansive that instead of traditional lighting, there were push-button timers that briefly illuminated several shelves of journals within the darkness. Without the light, I had no idea what was around me, and even when the light was on, I could see only the stacks directly in front of me.

Likewise, as we search through the library in our mind, we must carefully move from one section to the next. When we activate a cluster of neurons, those associations will light up only the ideas that are immediately connected. To reveal all that is truly there, we need patience and time. We need to explore systematically, searching the depths of our memory vault.

Look for a *Set* of Ideas

In 1968, Spencer Silver, a chemist at 3M, was attempting to develop a superstrong adhesive for use in aircraft construction. By accident, he discovered pretty much the opposite: a low-tack, reusable adhesive. The substance was pressure sensitive and could be easily removed without leaving residue. It could also be reused several times without losing its stickiness.

Silver was elated by his discovery—his colleagues less so. Despite the adhesive's unique properties, it didn't fit into any existing product categories. Silver himself could not come up with a clear practical application.

For five years, Silver brainstormed different possibilities, looking for any project at 3M that could make use of his adhesive. He even scheduled informal lunchtime talks to different departments, where, like a traveling salesperson, he pitched his adhesive to anyone who would listen. Eventually, a manager took a chance on one of Silver's ideas—an adhesive bulletin board where papers could be affixed and reaffixed.

Silver scheduled more lunchtime talks and began pitching the bulletin board idea internally. The bulletin board failed to catch on, but in one of those lunchtime talks, Silver's colleague Art Fry had a different thought. Fry sang in a church choir and regularly lost his hymn notes in his church songbook. He envisioned using Silver's adhesive to create a bookmark that would stay in place but could be repositioned without damaging the pages. Apply the adhesive to the paper, not the board. Together, Silver and Fry developed this concept into "Press 'n Peel" bookmarks.

Like the bulletin board, the bookmarks also failed. But Silver and Fry kept digging, exploring variations of office products that could use Silver's adhesive. Finally, they landed on Post-it Notes, which became one of 3M's most successful products. Through patient iteration, they had discovered a breakthrough idea hiding in plain sight.

The Post-it Notes story is often told as an example of grit and perseverance. Stay focused. Don't give up. With an optimistic mindset, anything is possible. But I think the 3M story is actually telling us something much deeper about the creative process. Namely, creative search is not about finding the right idea. It is about finding the right *set of ideas*.

Think about it: the bulletin board, the reusable bookmark, and reusable sticky notes are all variations of basically the same idea, paper + Silver's adhesive. We know that the bulletin board idea led to Press 'n Peel bookmarks, which led to Post-it Notes. But we can also easily imagine a world in which things didn't happen in this order at all.

Imagine, for example, if when Silver first discovered the adhesive, he accidentally stuck some pieces of paper together, realizing they could be attached and reattached. In that moment he could have seen the Post-it Note application. Or imagine if another one of Silver's colleagues recognized that the adhesive could be used on the back of tiny pieces of paper—maybe if they were an amateur artist who specialized in collage.

That's not what happened. But the point is that it could have. The potential was there, and that possibility illustrates what the act of Digging is truly accomplishing. It's about finding a promising area and thoroughly mining its possibilities. It is about identifying several ideas in a localized region with the hope that one "sticks."

This connects back to our earlier discussion of hot streaks (chapter 1)—those periods when creators seem to hit one success after another. When we look closely at these streaks, we often find they're not random bursts of inspiration but rather deep explorations of a promising space. Just as an artist might discover a compelling visual style that leads to multiple successful works, or an entrepreneur might identify a market need that spawns several successful products, Silver and Fry found themselves in a rich territory of possibility. The key was iterating and trying to narrow in. They couldn't know in advance whether the bulletin board, the bookmark, or the sticky note would be the version that would resonate with users. The only way forward was to explore them all.

Consider the Unexpected

Another strategy for how to dig for ideas comes from my colleague Samsun Knight, an economist and accomplished fiction author. In a 2024 paper, Knight and colleagues sought to answer an age-old question: What makes some narratives more compelling than others? The answer is *narrative reversals.*

Narrative reversals are the points at which a story's direction suddenly shifts, such as a dramatic change in a character's fortune or from good to bad. For example, Romeo and Juliet fall for each other at a masked ball only to realize that they are from feuding families; or, in *The Empire Strikes Back*, Darth Vader famously reveals to Luke Skywalker in the middle of a dramatic battle, "No, I am your father."

Knight and his colleagues analyzed nearly thirty thousand television shows, movies, and novels using a sophisticated computer algorithm. The results revealed that narratives with more reversals and larger reversals scored better with audiences, as measured by quantitative metrics like average star ratings from IMDB and the book sales of a novel. Put simply, the more narrative reversals a story has, the more audiences seem to enjoy it. Ideas that are counterintuitive or unexpected capture our attention in a unique way.

The insight here is that as we are looking for ideas, it may be helpful to focus on tensions—ideas that are surprising. But does this insight extend beyond the realm of narratives?

Knight and his colleagues also examined over a thousand fundraising pitches from the online fundraising platform GoFundMe. Each user's post on GoFundMe includes both a funding goal and a brief explanation of what the money is for. By analyzing these explanations, Knight's team found that narrative reversals also had a significant effect on fundraising. For example, successful backstories on GoFundMe were ones in which a person had been in a good situation only to find themselves suddenly on hard times, or conversely, when things had been quite difficult but now were suddenly improving. In fact, including reversals increased the probability of being funded by nearly 40%.

The catchiness of the unexpected is not limited to fiction and entertainment. It also seems to play a role in determining which real-world problems we find compelling and worthy of our attention.

Looking for reversals can be a powerful tool as we dig for ideas. One practical approach is to list our assumptions about a creative problem or topic area and then systematically ask: "What if the opposite were true?" These reversals often lead us to unexplored territory. Just as narrative reversals grab audience attention by defying expectations, hunting for counterintuitive or unexpected ideas can illuminate new paths forward, but only if we're willing to challenge our assumptions rigorously.

It's Never Too Late

The science of creativity tells us a lot about the search for ideas and where our instincts can mislead us. First, it shows the importance of persistence. Don't fall prey to the creative cliff illusion. Even though you may feel like you've exhausted every possible idea, that's usually a sign that the most promising ideas are ahead of you.

Second, Digging *is* a numbers game. More is more. Generate (what seems like) an obscene number of ideas—including lots of bad ones—to maximize your likelihood of success. Whatever seems like a reasonable number of ideas or a reasonable amount of time, double or even triple it.

Third, think about searching for the right set of ideas (not *the* right idea). Don't just stop when you find something you like. Instead, drill deeper to unearth several more ideas similar to the one you liked. Perhaps the most successful idea is right next to the idea you originally identified.

Fourth, think about tensions and reversals—what seems counterintuitive and unexpected. As you drill deeper, constantly be thinking of what the "opposite" or "reverse idea" would entail.

Which brings us to a final misconception that people have about creativity: If you don't have a great idea when you're young, then it's probably not going to happen.

In most cultures, there is a widespread belief that creativity declines with age. Youth is often associated with curiosity and mental flexibility, whereas older people are seen as resistant to change. As a result, people generally think that older people are less creative than younger people. Relatedly, because many people tend to endorse the notion of "creative genius," there is the belief that if a breakthrough hasn't happened while you are young and in your prime (cognitively speaking), it's unlikely to happen at all.

But this simply isn't true. If you look across dozens of studies that have examined the relationship between age and performance on a variety of creative tasks, there is no reliable effect. People do not get less creative as they age. For example, a study that asked participants to engage in a creative drawing task found no evidence of age differences in creativity. Other, more verbal tests of creativity also find no significant differences among people aged twenty-five to eighty-four in flexibility of thought, originality, or elaboration.

Some studies even find that people get more creative with age. Studies of creativity among older artists and architects found continuous improvement as they aged. And other research finds that older adults outperform younger adults on "everyday creativity" by adopting more problem-focused strategies and engaging in creative challenges with greater planning and efficiency.

And if you focus on just top achievers in a discipline (rather than the general population), the likelihood of having a breakthrough success also does not decrease with age. A study that looked at the careers of over six thousand film directors found no reliable relationship between a director's age and their likelihood of having a top-rated film. Among the directors who did have one or more breakthrough hits, those films were equally likely to occur at the beginning, middle, or end of the person's career.

Putting this together, we can make one more revision to people's common misconceptions about creativity: It's never too late. Keep searching. Whether it is a single session or a lifetime of work, there is always the possibility that your greatest discovery is in front of you.

Checklist for Effective Digging

Here is how to "set the stage" for effective Digging:

✓ **Prep Work:** Before you start any brainstorming process, make sure you have already done a lot of the prep work up front, including researching the topic extensively, engaging in high-resolution Surveying, defining a guiding question, and identifying relevant constraints.

✓ **Dedicate Time and Space:** Set aside time and space just for Digging. Commit yourself to focusing only on generating ideas.

✓ **Get Help:** Commit to spending some of your time Digging with others, including friends, collaborators, colleagues, and/or artificial intelligence (more on this in chapter 9).

✓ **Evaluation-Free Zone:** You (and others present) understand that the point of the exercise is simply to generate ideas, not evaluate them. In the next chapter, I provide several concrete strategies for how to do this.

✓ **Don't Rush**: Digging is a lengthy process of exploration, not something to be completed in ten or fifteen minutes. Think about idea generation as a continuous process that unfolds over days, weeks, or even months.

✓ **Record Everything**: Ensure that you have multiple ways of recording ideas as you generate them—make this as thoughtless and automatic as possible. All ideas count as progress. Ideas that are seemingly off topic, or unrealistic, or silly, are all great. No idea is bad.

✓ **Just Do It:** The act of Digging doesn't need to be precious or sacred—you are just searching. You don't have to be at your best. In fact, research suggests that people tend to be their most creative when they are *less* alert—being tired seems to encourage more creative leaps.

When you are searching for ideas, imagine that you are excavating with a shovel or tool. Just as you would constantly change the direction of your shovel to uncover new areas of terrain in different ways, you want to be thinking of regularly trying to shift your perspective and your process. And to do that, you will need to shake things up and see the creative challenge in new ways.

Experiment with generating ideas as if you were someone else—for example, "What ideas would my creative hero think of?" If you are brainstorming with others, experiment with different people, different group sizes, different pairings of individuals, and more. And make sure to change your physical location. Dig at home, at work, in transit, outside, in nature, in urban environments. As we discussed earlier, our physical environment can have a profound effect in spurring new thoughts and connections. You will be amazed at the difference in what you find by Digging in these different locations.

Remember: Just when you think you have exhausted all possible perspectives and approaches, that's probably when your process is starting to heat up!

Exercises

The exercises below are intended to help you push past the creative cliff and help you brainstorm in new ways by adopting different perspectives.

Exercise 20: Post-it Note Challenge

- **Gather multiple stacks of Post-it Notes** and a large surface for displaying ideas.

- **Write out your guiding question.**

- **Initial Session (Book 1).** Fill an entire book of Post-it Notes with ideas that answer your guiding question (there are one hundred Post-its in a book). Write down each idea that comes to mind on a separate Post-it. Aim for quantity—don't evaluate the ideas as you generate them. Simply try to use up the entire stack. Place each Post-it on a board or wall.

- **Take a break.** After returning, categorize the ideas into themes. Aim for at least three categories. Reflect on any emerging patterns.

- **Deep Dive Session (Book 2).** Dedicate time (over multiple days) to further idea generation. Over the course of subsequent sessions, aim to fill an entire second book of Post-it Notes with ideas and add them to the board. Add ideas to the existing categories and/or generate ideas in a totally new category. Don't forget to consult outside resources.

- **Two hundred ideas may seem like a lot.** It is. But that is the point. By setting a very high bar you will force yourself to look past the obvious, push through the creative cliff, and make new associations and connections that you wouldn't have otherwise.

Exercise 21: Idea Tweaks

The goal of this exercise is to think about generating a constellation (or set) of related ideas. To do so, focus on a single promising idea and then think about different ways of tweaking it slightly.

- **Selection.** Pick an idea that you find particularly exciting or promising.

- **Now start thinking of different ways you could slightly alter or tweak the idea:**
    1. **Add an element:** Introduce something new. How does it change the idea?
    2. **Remove an element:** Strip something away. Does the core concept survive or evolve?
    3. **Swap it:** Replace a key feature with something else. What shifts?
    4. **Expand it:** Make the idea ten times bigger in scale, scope, or impact.
    5. **Make it niche:** Adapt it for a highly specific audience. Who, and why?
    6. **Invert it:** Reverse a core assumption. What unexpected version emerges?
    7. **Shrink it, blow it up:** What happens when it's tiny? Enormous?

8. **Make it for the "wrong" audience:** Who would never use this? And how could they?

9. **Time travel it:** How would this idea work in the past? The distant future?

10. **Break a rule:** Violate an unspoken norm. What doors does that open?

11. **Give it a personality:** If this idea were a person, what would its desires and quirks be? What would the idea look like as a different person?

12. **Force a clash:** Merge this idea with something wildly unrelated. What sparks?

Exercise 22: Ideas from the Future

The goal of this exercise is to generate ideas by imagining yourself in the future, looking back on having successfully completed the project.

- **Imagine yourself in the future** once you have discovered the perfect solution to your creative problem. First, how does it feel now that you've accomplished it? And looking back, what did it take to get there?

- **Generate ideas from the perspective of your future self.** What does the solution look like? Write down every idea.

- **Review the ideas and reflect** on any new patterns or promising directions. Consider how adopting this backward-looking perspective influenced your thinking.

Exercise 23: Bad Ideas

Sometimes, the worst ideas can lead to the best insights. In this exercise, the goal is to deliberately brainstorm bad ideas.

- **Start with your guiding question.**

- **Now come up with terrible ideas.** Let go of any filters. Aim for ideas that are the absolute worst—ridiculous, impractical, or counterproductive. For example, if you are brainstorming how to make your daily work meetings shorter, begin by brainstorming how to make them *longer*.

- **Write down every bad idea**, no matter how absurd it seems.

- **Go through each bad idea and consider why it doesn't work.** Is there a kernel of truth or an interesting angle hidden within it?

- **Now take some of the worst ideas and flip them.** How might you reverse or tweak them into more productive, innovative solutions?

- **Finally, review both your bad and flipped ideas.** Highlight any concepts that seem interesting or worth exploring further. Sometimes, the wildest bad ideas contain the seeds of breakthrough solutions.

8.

Search Far and Wide

In 1993, Icelandic musician Björk released *Debut*—an eclectic mix of electronica, world music, and pop. The album quickly climbed the charts, and within months it was on track to sell a million copies. By all accounts, *Debut* was a breakout success.

From there, Björk built one of the most enduring and celebrated careers in music, recording nine more studio albums, with eight consecutively reaching the Billboard Top 20. She's composed film scores, pushed artistic boundaries, and won many prestigious awards, including the Polar Music Prize, often called the "Nobel Prize of music."

But Björk's *Debut* wasn't really a debut at all. By the time her album was released, she had already lived several musical lives. Björk recorded her first album at just eleven years old, after being discovered singing at a school recital. A few years later, she formed the all-female punk group Spit and Snot. At fifteen, she began experimenting with jazz fusion in bands like Exodus and Jam-80. She played drums in the art-rock band Rokka Rokka Drum and fronted eclectic post-punk groups like Tappi Tíkarrass and Kukl. By her early twenties, her main band, the Sugarcubes, gained international attention with their single

"Birthday." In fact, several of the songs on *Debut* were written years earlier during her time in these other bands.

In this chapter, we'll see why this type of creative exploration is so important. The research suggests that when individuals experiment—searching far and wide—they build a rich portfolio of skills that they can draw from later.

In Björk's case, her early exploration in many musical genres may be one of the key factors that contributed to her sustained success. As she told *The Creative Independent*, "I think also maybe because I was in bands from 13 or 12 . . . all I did was write melodies and lyrics. I think that just became something I could do while I was raising a child or [on] shopping errands or doing a normal daily-life routine."

Across fields, the most successful creatives tend to cast a wide net. Musicians, Nobel Prize winners, and even Olympic athletes have benefitted from experimenting broadly. That early range doesn't just shape what you know. It shapes who you meet, how you think, and what kinds of approaches you're able to pursue later. An expansive mindset—one that favors range and experimentation—is one of the most powerful ways to dig deeper, generate more, and follow your first big hit with another.

The Secret to Sustained Success

Justin Berg is a professor of organizational behavior at the University of Michigan, where he studies creativity and innovation. His research has tackled a number of fascinating questions, including one that has long baffled academics and nonacademics alike: Why do some musicians become one-hit wonders—having only one commercial breakthrough—while others have sustained success?

The question is puzzling: Given the ability to write at least one popular song, why do some artists disappear? Conventional wisdom points to all sorts of potential explanations: the pressures of fame, fickle tastes of the public, perhaps just bad luck. But Berg's research shows that the key to breaking the curse of the one-hit wonder may have less to do with what happens after you have your big hit and instead everything to do with what happens *before* it.

To answer the question of what leads to sustained success, Berg embarked on an ambitious analysis. He assembled a massive dataset of every piece of recorded Western pop music he could get his hands on. The final tally was a staggering three million songs by nearly seventy thousand artists. For each artist, Berg analyzed their entire catalog: the songs they recorded before their first hit, their breakthrough moments on the Billboard Top 100, and everything that came after.

Then, using sophisticated algorithms to analyze musical style and genre across those millions of songs, Berg discovered something remarkable. The key predictor of whether an artist has multiple hits isn't timing, or their genre, or their label. Instead, it was variety—specifically, how much the artist had experimented with different musical styles before they became famous. Artists who tried their hand at different musical genres before their big break were far more likely to have sustained success compared to those who had focused more narrowly.

Consider Janet Jackson, another artist who, like Björk, has had a remarkable string of hits. Following her breakthrough album *Control* (1982), Jackson had forty-two Top 100 hits. But contrary to popular belief, *Control* was not Jackson's debut—it was actually her third album. Before her big breakthrough, Jackson had experimented with a variety of styles, including pop, dance, R&B, soul, and funk. This early exploration gave her the versatility she would later need to continuously evolve her sound.

This pattern—call it the power of *early diversification*—shows up far beyond the music industry. If you compare Olympic medalists to other elite athletes who competed but didn't medal, you see that as children, the medalists spent significantly more time playing multiple sports and less time specializing in their primary sport. The same is true for scientists. When you compare Nobel laureates to other highly accomplished researchers, you find that the Nobel winners were more likely to have worked across different disciplines early in their careers.

Why is early diversification so powerful? For one, it allows people to develop a larger portfolio of skills that they can draw from, kind of like a Swiss Army knife. For the musicians in Berg's study, artists that experimented before they got famous were able to pivot to a different genre if their original style of music became unpopular.

Second, early diversification can provide general knowledge or expertise that applies to lots of different contexts. In learning to write songs in multiple genres, you may gain insights about songwriting more generally.

And finally, when people engage in early diversification, they are more likely to find the thing that "clicks" with their unique talents and interests. As a result, individuals who have engaged in early diversification may be better matched to their area of professional specialization.

But this type of diversification doesn't occur in a vacuum. We're social creatures, and our early explorations are shaped by the connections we make and the environments we inhabit. A musician typically doesn't just wake up one day and decide to experiment with jazz fusion or math rock. These explorations emerge naturally from crossing paths with other musicians or by getting pulled into unexpected collaborations. Similarly, when scientists branch out into a new area, it usually starts with a conversations over coffee or a workshop.

The point is that early diversification isn't a solo exercise. It's inherently social. The breadth of your early experimentation depends largely on the breadth of your connections. And as we'll see, the breadth of our social networks can expand our creative horizons in ways we might never expect.

The Power of Weak Ties

Since the mid-2000s, Korean pop music (or K-pop) has slowly taken over the world. But behind every K-pop supergroup, like BTS or Blackpink, is a vast network of some ten thousand songwriters and producers. This creative ecosystem might have remained invisible if not for a unique opportunity. The South Korean government maintains a database of every song, from every Korean artist, in ever genre, that has ever been recorded. It's the complete history of Korean music and musicians.

Sociologists Yonghoon Lee and Martin Gargiulo managed to get their hands on this treasure trove of data and mapped out this entire ecosystem of K-pop songwriters. Who collaborated with whom? When did they work together? What was the effect of those collaborations? By analyzing the data in this way, they were able to reconstruct the entire network, observing how it grew and morphed over time. The patterns they uncovered tell an intriguing story.

Like most professionals, K-pop songwriters typically start their careers in small, tight-knit circles. And as their careers progress, those networks grow and become more diverse and open. This follows a natural progression: The longer you spend in an industry, the more people you meet, creating more opportunities for collaboration.

But here's where it gets interesting: When Lee and Gargiulo analyzed what distinguished the most successful songwriters (those with multiple hits) from their less successful peers, they found that the hitmakers "opened" their networks faster. These songwriters were more aggressive about making connections to distant songwriters outside their initial network. Crucially, because this network expansion happened *before* people's big hits, it wasn't simply that these songwriters had more opportunities after becoming famous. Long before their breakthrough moments, these future success stories were actively forging new connections and widening their social networks.

This finding dovetails perfectly with one of sociology's most influential ideas, the "strength of weak ties" proposed by Mark Granovetter.

The strength of a tie between two people is exactly what it sounds like. Strong ties are characterized by frequent interaction, high trust, and reciprocity—think of your best friend, life partner, or close family member. Weak ties, on the other hand, are your acquaintances, friends of friends—people you know but not well. Everyone in your life falls somewhere along this strong-to-weak tie continuum.

The benefits of strong ties are obvious. These are the people we turn to for emotional support who provide our sense of belonging. But when and why are weak ties beneficial? Granovetter argued that it boils down to information. Essentially, your strong ties have much of the same information that you do: You've had the same experiences (probably together), watched and read many of the same things; you might have gone to the same schools or work in the same place. It is well documented that a person's similarity to you is probably one of the main reasons why they are a strong tie in the first place. We are naturally drawn to people who are like us.

And yet this similarity can backfire when it comes to creativity. Returning to our excavation analogy, searching for ideas with a strong tie is a bit like Digging with an extra set of hands. Your strong tie is seeing all the same things you are, searching for ideas in all the same places, reacting to potential discoveries in the same way. Sure, an extra set of hands can be great to help speed things along. But if the name of the game is to try to cover as much ground as possible and unearth all that you can, you are better-off partnering with someone who knows different things than you do and sees the world differently. That's where weak ties come in: They have access to different information and networks, which helps expand the search for new ideas in unexpected directions.

In the years since Granovetter proposed this theory, numerous studies have validated his predictions about the importance of weak ties for creativity. One such example is a large-scale analysis of five million scientific papers. It showed that research teams connected by weak ties produced more impactful work than did teams bound by strong ties alone. Similarly, when managers at a large company evaluated hundreds of work teams, breakthrough ideas came more frequently from teams that included weak ties across diverse departments.

When the Going Gets Tough, Don't Turtle Up

Interestingly, when people encounter setbacks, creative blocks, or failures, research shows that their knee-jerk response is not to turn to their weak ties, but instead to rely on their strong-tie network. A study of millions of instant messages on LinkedIn, for example, found that in times of business distress and economic downturn, people were more likely to message those in their immediate network. The authors cleverly named this phenomenon "turtling-up."

From an emotional viewpoint, this makes complete sense. When life is tough, we want to get support and help from our closest friends. But from the perspective of creativity and information sharing, this might be the exact wrong approach.

When we hit creative blocks, the answer is not to climb inside our shell and look inward. Rather, we must reorient, face outward, and to the best of our ability seek new kinds of information and ideas. Whereas a close friend can offer a sympathetic shoulder, the spark of

If you hit a creative block, resist the urge to shrink your social network.

your next breakthrough idea is more likely to come from a friend of a friend.

The takeaway from this research is remarkably similar to the advice we have seen already: There are enormous benefits from drawing on as many resources as you can. Diversify as much as possible. Dig lots of holes. And the earlier you start "expanding" in this way—both in terms of exposure to ideas and weak ties in your social network—the better.

Boosting Your Collective Intelligence

So far, we've explored creativity through the lens of networks and connections. But what happens when we zoom in? What makes some small groups more creative than others?

In a fascinating series of experiments, psychologists at Carnegie Mellon University and MIT had people complete a battery of intelligence and personality tests. Then all those same people were randomly assigned to teams of five. Together, the teams tackled a range of creative challenges, from brainstorming to design tasks.

When the researchers analyzed the data—both the individual assessments as well as the collective performance of the group—they found that the team's performance was not simply the sum of its members' abilities. In fact, even having an exceptionally intelligent person on the team didn't guarantee better results. Instead, the researchers uncovered something they called "collective intelligence": the group's ability to work together effectively. This single factor explained nearly half of what made teams successful.

What causes collective intelligence? It seems to boil down to two key factors. The first is emotional intelligence. Teams whose members were better at reading and responding to one another's social cues performed better as a group.

The second factor was more surprising: turn-taking. The most successful teams weren't dominated by one or two voices. Instead, they actively solicited ideas from everyone. Interestingly, there was actually a third factor that positively predicted collective intelligence, which was the number of women in the group. However, this effect was explained by the fact that women tend to score higher on measures of emotional intelligence and engage in more turn-taking.

If creativity really is a numbers game, then the benefits of soliciting as many ideas as you can from as many different sources as you can far outweigh the costs. Of course, not all ideas will be gems. But what the collective intelligence research tells us is that even the smartest people in the room (or on the team) do not necessarily know best. So then, why not hear everyone out? Why not let the creative process unfold, and meander, and heat up? All this requires is a bit of patience, withholding skepticism, and recognizing that we are all engaged in the same process of Digging and discovery.

This might sound idealistic given the realities of most workplaces—

where someone needs to make final decisions and keep projects on track. But it is entirely doable. Below, I have included several practical strategies for how to unearth everything you can from the collective and ensure that you're hearing from everyone:

Make Digging evaluation-free. This is perhaps the most important advice: While you're generating ideas, don't allow evaluations to creep in. Instead, the goal is to be as positive and forward-looking as possible. No idea is a bad idea because at this point, there is no good or bad.

It helps to say explicitly, "We are not evaluating ideas" before any brainstorming begins. Then, throughout the Digging session, gently reinforce the norm that the time is about discovering ideas, not evaluating them. And it might mean that the skeptical curmudgeons in the room—whose critique and insights will be invaluable at the Sifting stage—need reminding of the goals at hand.

I used to take part in a lab meeting that was attended by PhD students as well as several professors. The main goal of this meeting was for graduate students to brainstorm early-stage ideas. However, several of the professors had trouble suspending their criticism during those meetings, and the effects were all too predictable. The students stopped sharing. No one would present anything unless it was in a final, polished state.

Eventually we realized that the meeting had become ineffective, and we implemented a new solution: a squirt gun. When simple reminders to withhold critiques failed, we resorted to spraying.

Separate Digging from Sifting. Set aside dedicated time to dig, and dig only. Make the number of ideas, rather than the quality of ideas, your target. It can also be helpful to have a dedicated space. In previous chapters, we discussed the benefits of external stimulation on creativity, so don't be afraid to mix it up and try Digging in new and different locations: in nature, an art museum, or at the airport. Experiment with different combinations of people. Generate ideas as a group, then individually, then in pairs, then in small clusters. Experiment with the order of these activities. Imagine you and your team as excavators of conceptual space, trying to unearth every inch of the terrain.

Formalize turn-taking. In group discussions, people—especially the introverts—spend mental energy worrying about how to avoid talking over others or when is their "right time" to contribute. That's energy that could be better spent engaging with ideas. While it might feel a bit artificial at first, implementing a formal turn-taking system can eliminate these distractions. When everyone knows they'll have dedicated time to speak, there's no need to compete for airtime or strategically time comments. Quieter voices aren't overshadowed, and each person knows their turn will come.

This can also have a secondary benefit in enhancing accountability. When everyone knows they will have to chime in, hanging back isn't an option. That added pressure can sometimes be the perfect catalyst for sparking a new and completely different line of thinking.

Consider using simple tools like a deck of cards or a random-number generator to make the order in which people speak random. An element of chance can prevent people from slipping into familiar patterns.

Make submissions anonymous. Ever notice how people become comedic geniuses in anonymous comment sections? There's something liberating about throwing ideas into the ring without your name attached. Suddenly, that wild idea doesn't seem so crazy. Digital tools, note cards, or even the old-school "put it in a hat" method can transform hesitant contributors into idea-generating machines. The best part? When an idea does win over the room, you can be sure that it was based purely on its own merit rather than on who pitched it.

Purposely generate bad ideas. Deliberately soliciting ideas that seem impractical or even absurd can, paradoxically, lead to breakthrough insights. These seemingly poor ideas often contain unexpected nuggets of wisdom that can be stepping stones to finding something great. Also, the permission to share bad ideas helps break down the perfectionism that can paralyze idea generation. When people feel free to share ideas that will be rejected, they often find that what initially seemed ridiculous contains valuable elements that can be refined or combined with other concepts.

Let someone else lead. Having junior (or typically quieter) people lead brainstorming sessions can have multiple benefits. This role reversal not only empowers new voices; it can also help senior members step back from their usual decision-making positions. Freed from the responsibility of directing the conversation, the go-to ringleader might feel more license to contribute freely as a participant.

Sometimes the solution is to switch places literally. My friend, social psychologist Adam Galinsky, noticed that during research meetings, his student would barely speak, instead spending the whole time furiously taking notes. One day, on a whim, he had the student sit in his "professor chair" behind the desk. The transformation was immediate: The student began to engage actively, even challenging some of the professor's assumptions. What changed? Simply by occupying the physical space of authority, the student felt empowered to contribute as an equal. Often the key to unlocking great ideas is to have the usual decision-makers take a step back from the head of the table.

Use the "yes, and" strategy. One of the biggest barriers to effective brainstorming is that people often aren't truly listening to others' ideas. Instead, they're mentally rehearsing what they want to say next.

A technique borrowed from improv comedy offers an elegant solution. Called "yes, and," the approach is simple: Take each idea, accept it, and use it as a springboard to something new. Make it a rule that everyone must build on someone else's contribution before pitching their own. When practiced, this approach can start a chain reaction where each idea sparks the next. Even better, hearing ideas repeated and reframed often reveals new possibilities that weren't obvious the first time around.

Are Virtual Teams As Creative?

I'm often asked if virtual meetings are as effective for creativity as in-person collaborations. Most people intuitively feel that they're not, that there's something special about all being in the same room, and research backs that up. But here's the twist: Virtual teams aren't less creative because of stilted conversation or lagging energy. They're less creative because they're too focused.

In 2022, Melanie Brucks and Jonathan Levav, psychologists at Stanford University, recruited fifteen hundred product engineers from a large company. The engineers were paired off and asked to generate new product ideas. Half the teams met in person. The other half collaborated over video. As expected, the in-person teams produced more ideas, and their ideas were rated as more successful by independent evaluators.

But the question is *why?*

The researchers reviewed video recordings and confirmed what most of us might suspect: Virtual collaboration felt awkward, people talked over each other, the rhythm was off. But those hiccups didn't explain the creativity gap. The real explanation emerged only after the researchers used sophisticated eye-tracking software to analyze where people had been looking during the sessions.

When people met in person, they didn't stare at each other the whole time. Their eyes wandered—to the walls, the floor, the furniture, the view outside. And that visual drifting predicted which teams were more creative. The more people looked around, the better their ideas. It was *distraction* that fueled their creativity.

This might sound counterintuitive at first, but it fits perfectly with the discovery mindset we've been exploring. Even highly trained professionals don't just generate ideas from within. They draw on their environment: a tree, a weird-looking piece of furniture. These stray stimuli give the mind something to bounce off. But in virtual settings, people stay locked on the screen; it feels rude not to. As a result, their brainstorming stays locked in too.

The good news? This is fixable. Virtual collaboration isn't doomed, it's just impoverished. If you want to unlock more creativity online, don't just stare at the screen. Let your eyes wander. Place something strange in your field of view. Embrace the distractions. When you let your eyes start to drift, just don't forget to say, "Excuse me. I'm not ignoring you. I'm trying to enhance our creative output!"

Picture brainstorming like an excavation site, rich with potential but also uncertain. To discover something great, you must dig in multiple places, at different depths, and with varied tools. But Digging alone is often not enough. The true power of your efforts lies in the network you cultivate—connections to people and ideas that stretch beyond what's familiar and comfortable. It's through these weak ties, these seemingly tenuous threads, that you gain access to new perspectives, fresh ideas, and the serendipitous collisions that spark innovation. When you find yourself stuck, resist the urge to retreat inward. Instead, search far and wide. The inspiration you need is often just beyond your current comfort zone.

Exercises

The aim of these exercises is to inspire group creativity, leveraging the benefits of collective intelligence and weak ties.

Exercise 24: King of the Mountain

This is a collaborative exercise designed to refine ideas through multiple rounds of focused Digging.

- **The Team.** Get together with one to three other people, ideally outside your immediate circle.

- **Define the Challenge.** Clearly articulate the specific challenge or project through a guiding question. Write it in a place where everyone can see it, such as on a board or projector.

- **Initial Idea Generation.** Each participant on their own generates and writes down as many ideas as possible on separate Post-it Notes or pieces of paper. Set a timer if that's helpful. At the end of the round, each participant reviews their own Post-its and selects their **top two ideas** and places them on the board/wall. Remove any duplicates.
  - □ **Move best ideas to the top.** All participants discuss the ideas and anonymously vote on their favorites. Move the top three ideas to the top of the mountain. Take care not to let any one person decide which ideas are on top.

- **Second Round.** Participants brainstorm new ideas, writing down as many as they can. At the end of the round, each participant selects their **top two ideas** and adds them to the board. Remove any duplicates.

- ▫ **Move best ideas to the top.** All participants discuss the ideas and anonymously vote on their favorites (could be ideas from round 1 or 2). Move the top three ideas to the top of the mountain.

- **Recording/Reflection**
  - ▫ Be sure to record (photograph) each stage. Take notes and discuss the "king of the mountain" ideas, but save all ideas generated from all rounds.
  - ▫ Leave time to discuss any unselected ideas that were generated but not posted.

Exercise 25: Engaging Your Weak Ties

- **Make a list** of all the people you can think of in your current professional and personal networks (friends, friends of friends, colleagues, family members, social media connections).

- **Categorize each person as a strong or weak tie.** Recall, strong ties are characterized by a lot of time spent interacting—think of your close friends, family members, or colleagues you see regularly. For weak ties, think acquaintances, friends of friends, people you know but not very well.

- **Review your list of weak ties** and identify anyone who may have interesting connections to your project.

- **Organize an informal conversation with a weak tie.** Explain your project and guiding question, but don't tell them anything else. Wait for their first thoughts about your project.

9.

The Spark

Guernica, by Pablo Picasso, is considered one of the most powerful paintings in Western art. Spanning more than 25 feet in length, the painting captures the terror and chaos of a single day: April 26, 1937. On that day, German warplanes—acting on behalf of Francisco Franco's Nationalist forces—bombed the town of Guernica, Spain, while its citizens shopped in the open-air market. Hundreds were killed. The town was decimated.

At the time of the bombing, Picasso was living in Paris, working on a large mural for the 1937 World's Fair. He had been chipping away for months, making little progress. When news of the bombing reached him, Picasso was devastated. Almost immediately, he set to work on *Guernica*.

Interestingly, all the preparatory sketches that Picasso made for *Guernica* have been carefully preserved—everything from the drawings he made just after hearing about the bombing to the ones he made while finalizing the work. Together, they provide a rare glimpse into Picasso's process, telling a remarkable story about how great ideas emerge and how they evolve.

One striking insight from these sketches is that many visual elements in *Guernica* can be traced back to earlier works. For example, the twisted, anguished faces echo Francisco Goya's *Disasters of War*. And many of the main characters in *Guernica* bear a striking resemblance to *Minotauromachy* (1935), an etching Picasso had made a few years earlier. *Guernica* even contains an object resembling a newspaper clipping, perhaps a reference to Picasso learning of the tragedy. Consistent with themes we've explored throughout this book, Picasso's sketches suggest that he drew heavily from his external environment and what had come before.

But an even more startling insight is just how much of the final composition was there from the start, even the very first sketch: the anguished horse at the painting's center, the outstretched arms, the screaming figures, even the basic layout. It's almost as if the idea arrived fully formed in the moment that Picasso first heard of the bombing. And as Picasso refined the painting, that initial spark seemed to guide his process. As creativity scholar Robert Weisberg writes, "[Picasso's] thought did not range in a free manner over the entire universe of materials . . . he worked systematically . . . the elaboration of a kernel idea."

This second point is important because it challenges a common misconception about creativity. Maybe you've heard phrases like "Execution is everything" or "Ideas are cheap; it's hard work that matters." Platitudes like these would have us think that the idea itself is not as important as the time and effort we put in to realize it. But what made *Guernica* such an extraordinary achievement wasn't just Picasso's technical skill or persistence; it was also the clarity and power of the raw idea.

Indeed, a striking feature of many creative breakthroughs is the extent to which the very first instantiation of the idea—the initial *spark*—already contains many of the elements that later make it great. As the renowned filmmaker David Lynch put it,

> *We don't really create an idea. We just catch them like fish. No chef ever takes credit for making the fish. It's just preparing the fish. So, you get an idea and it is like a seed. . . . Then the thing is translating that idea to some medium.*

But people often fail to appreciate this fact. Instead, they settle for mediocre ideas, believing that in the end, hard work and execution will save the day.

I've personally witnessed a version of this in my own class. I ask my students to form groups and complete a semester-long research project. After students submit their projects, I ask them about how they came up with their idea. I'm always struck by how most groups finalize their topic during their very first meeting, often within the first few minutes. The majority of their time and effort goes to executing the idea.

In this chapter, we'll see why this is a mistake. We'll review fascinating research that shows how the raw idea has a surprisingly large impact on a project's success. We'll also see how waiting until we find the right idea can have additional benefits, like streamlining implementation, leading to less work overall. Finally, we'll discuss how generative artificial intelligence (AI) is playing an increasingly important role in helping creatives of all types unearth those promising sparks.

What once took days or weeks can now be done in a fraction of the time. We'll examine how today's creatives are using this powerful technology not just to generate more ideas but also to find the ones worth pursuing.

Good Ideas Are Worth Waiting For

In his illuminating book *On Writing*, author Stephen King describes how he came up with the idea for *Misery*. He was flying to London and awoke from a strange dream about a psychotic fan of a popular writer. On the back of an American Airlines napkin he wrote,

> *She speaks earnestly but never quite makes eye contact. A big woman and solid all through; she is an absence of hiatus. "I wasn't trying to be funny in a mean way when I named my pig Misery, no sir. Please don't think that. No, I named her in the spirit of fan love which is the purest love there is. You should be flattered."*

And that was it. That was the spark, the kernel of an idea that later became one of King's best-selling novels.

When King landed in London, he asked the hotel concierge for a place to work and was led to a desk once used by the nineteenth-century author Rudyard Kipling. King recalls, "When I sat down at Mr. Kipling's beautiful desk I had the basic situation—crippled writer, psycho fan—firmly fixed in my mind. The actual *story* did not exist, well it did, but as a relic buried . . . in the earth. . . . I had located the fossil; the rest, I knew, would consist of careful excavation."

King then describes a very similar phenomenon to "When Stories Write Themselves," discussed in chapter 5, where the characters began to take control. "Paul Sheldon [the writer] turned out to be a good deal more resourceful than I initially thought. . . . Annie [his psychotic captor] also turned out to be more complex than I'd first imagined her, and she was great fun to write about. . . . And none of the story's details and incidents proceeded from plot; they were organic, each arising naturally from the initial situation, each an uncovered part of the fossil."

King's experience writing *Misery*—from the moment of inspiration on the plane to the gradual unearthing of his characters—illustrates how the initial spark of an idea often carries enormous weight in shaping the final outcome of creative work. King didn't need the entire plot mapped out in detail from the start; rather, it was the core concept that propelled the story forward.

We also see versions of this in very different domains, like the invention of consumer products. Consider a fascinating study that analyzed years' worth of data from a website called Quirky.com. Quirky is a crowdsourced platform that solicits ideas from budding inventors. Typically, the products are items that retail for $150 or less—things like reimagined staplers, wallet-sized padlocks, or desk storage devices for pens and paintbrushes.

Quirky runs a weekly contest in which members on the site vote for their favorite product ideas. Submitted ideas need to consist of only a sketch or two and a brief description. The ideas that get the most votes are then turned into real products.

But it isn't the original creator who is in charge. It's the other members on the site and employees at Quirky who refine that concept, create renderings, test materials, and name it. Eventually, the product is manufactured and sold, with a percentage of royalties going to the creators as well as the other members who helped refine the product.

What this means—and what makes Quirky unique from a research standpoint—is that ideation (coming up with the idea) and implementation (actually making it) are kept completely separate, performed by two completely different groups. It's a bit like if my students came up with the topic idea for their projects, but then they handed that raw idea off to a completely different group of students to actually complete it and submit it for a grade.

The question is, Which matters more for success, the idea itself or how it is implemented?

Researchers Laura Kornish and Karl Ulrich got ahold of many products that had appeared on Quirky.com, both the initial sketches and the final products. Then they took all those ideas to a panel of experts who independently rated their market potential. Some experts rated the idea in its raw form, while others rated the final product.

What they found was surprising: Ratings of the raw idea were equally as predictive of the product's actual market success as were ratings of the final product. In other words, much like the Picasso painting or King's *Misery*, the relative "greatness" of the product ideas on Quirky were evident in the very first instantiation, even just a rough sketch. This finding suggests that the core strength of an idea is present in its earliest form before any refinement or development takes place.

More Time Searching = Less Time Overall

You may think that spending more time searching for an idea means that you've simply added more work to your plate. After all, there are many steps to transform that initial idea into a final product. But even though better ideas can take longer to find, they often take considerably *less* time to develop. More time searching can actually mean less work overall.

There are dozens of anecdotes from accomplished artists, musicians, and authors who talk about how quickly their career-making hit came together after arriving at the initial spark. Nina Simone wrote "Mississippi Goddam" in less than an hour after hearing about the Birmingham church bombing. Paul McCartney wrote "Yesterday" in a matter of minutes after awaking from a dream. Taylor Swift wrote "We Are Never Ever Getting Back Together" in about twenty-five minutes. When John Boyne came up with the idea of his Holocaust-based story *The Boy in the Striped Pajamas*, he finished it in under a week.

Amy Tan drafted *The Joy Luck Club* in just four months after the concept crystallized. The list goes on.

Again and again, creators say the same thing when asked about their great work: Once they landed on the right idea, the process of bringing it to fruition was effortless and seemingly self-guided. From the initial spark, everything else flowed almost effortlessly, as if the idea itself knew what it wanted to become.

Why? Think back to our discussion about constraints in chapter 5. Great sparks don't just hint in a vague direction. They cue something specific and complex—a self-contained universe with a core idea, a set of satellite concepts, a mood, emotions, an energy, and flow.

Like Stephen King's spark that led to *Misery*, read it again and see how much richness is there: setting, motivation, deep layers of personality and meaning. It is that internal structure contained in the *spark* that propels things forward and makes us feel as if we are unearthing something that has always been there. Our unconscious mind has glimpsed the idea and what it could become, and now begins the careful work of unearthing it.

This realization reinforces a major theme from this section on Digging: There is significant value in simply persisting in the idea-generation stage. What might feel like wasted time searching is often repaid many times over in the smooth execution that follows. A strong spark sets the boundaries of possibility, shaping the choices you'll make as you refine and execute your idea. Taking the time to uncover something extraordinary establishes the foundation that propels the rest of your creative process forward.

Using AI to Discover Sparks

So how do we find those sparks? The history of creativity is filled with tales of long walks, hot showers, and fitful dreams. More recently, though, some creators have begun turning to generative artificial intelligence (AI), not to replace those moments, but to accelerate their arrival.

I'm not going to suggest that human and AI creativity are the same—they're not. AI's creativity is purely computational, whereas human creativity isn't just cognitive. It's also emotional, personal, self-reflective, cultural, and more. What we create has meaning to us in a sense that doesn't exist for artificial intelligence. Nonetheless, it is important to understand where and how new AI tools can help us—especially when it comes to finding a spark that we can develop into something great.

Although most of us don't have specialized knowledge of the inner workings of AI, we can still understand its "creativity" in broad strokes: A system of rules governs inputs and outputs, an underlying logic allows for the combination of basic elements, and there's a healthy dose of trial and error. Some of what AI comes up with will strike us as interesting, useful, or beautiful. Most will not.

However, when we begin to unpack AI's creativity a bit more, notice how much of its method overlaps with many of the principles in this book.

Consider InnoVAE, an AI developed by a team of computer scientists at Boston University. The researchers gave InnoVAE text from 600,000 US technology patents, representing some of the most transformative technologies in recent history—innovations like the Google PageRank algorithm and the iPhone touch screen. Then they asked InnoVAE to come up with a system for organizing all those patents.

How does a computer do this? Imagine, for example, if someone asked you to organize a chest of old photographs. After laying out all the photos, you would start to notice elements the photos had in common: Is the photo black-and-white or color? Was it taken outside or inside? Does it contain people, animals, natural formations?

In a similar fashion, InnoVAE looked at its trove of patents and began to extract the primary ways in which the patents varied. This allowed InnoVAE to assign each of the 600,000 patents a location in multidimensional space similar to a geocoordinate—just (try to) imagine twelve dimensions instead of two.

Now, the fun part. InnoVAE began to crawl through the conceptual space, defined by the grid, searching for new ideas. It found ideas like a method for detecting counterfeit tampering of portable electronic devices; a method for automatically generating a graphical user interface; and in a rather spooky twist of meta-awareness, an idea for a technology company that would use AI to generate technology patents.

What's fascinating here isn't just the ideas InnoVAE generated but how it found them. Much like an explorer charting unknown territory, InnoVAE first created a map of existing ideas and then systematically ventured into unexplored areas to discover new possibilities. In short, InnoVAE's process is remarkably similar to the steps of Surveying, Gridding, and Digging that we have been discussing.

This pattern—of mapping a creative space and then methodically exploring it—appears in other domains of AI creativity as well. Take humor, for instance.

One of the creative tasks I use in my lab is to have people write jokes. Participants are shown cartoons and asked to come up with funny captions, much like the popular *New Yorker* cartoon contest. Recently, I wondered, *Could AI perform this same task? Could it be funny?*

To find out, I showed the same cartoon to both humans and GPT-4: an image of two businesspeople sitting in a boat, stranded in the middle of a lake. I then asked my participants and GPT to come up with captions to fit the cartoon. I gave all those jokes to a different group of people who rated how funny they were without knowing which were created by humans and which by AI.

Both people and AI produced some genuinely funny captions, but there were telling differences in how they approached the task. AI consistently gravitated toward puns. For example, *"When they said the com-*

pany was going under, I didn't expect this," or *"I guess this is one way to test the waters with a new business model."* Humans, while occasionally using puns, showed more variety: *"I know this isn't a good time, but I'm going to need December 12th off,"* or *"This meeting could have been an email."*

But here's what was particularly interesting: It took more than a thousand people, each generating multiple jokes, to arrive at the best human-created jokes. GPT-4, in contrast, produced a set of equally highly rated jokes in matter of seconds.

This highlights a crucial pattern we see across creative domains. AI excels at rapidly exploring defined creative spaces, while humans are necessary for providing guidance and curation.

The Value of AI Comes from Guidance and Curation

To illustrate, consider a fascinating study that examined how AI has impacted digital artwork. Led by Dokyun Lee at Boston University (one of the same researchers who created InnoVAE), the researchers analyzed a database of four million pieces of digital art submitted by fifty thousand different artists.

Here were the top-line results: In general, the use of AI (to date) has led to *less* interesting art. On average, artists who use AI tend to produce work that is more homogenous and less original compared to artists who don't. But also consistent with a "more is more" approach, artists who use AI generate substantially more material than artists who don't use AI. And that increase in productivity means a higher likelihood of producing work that others rate as good.

In other words, collaborating with AI increases artists' output. On average, that output is less original (than when people don't use AI), but occasionally collaborating with AI produces something notable that people would have been less likely to achieve on their own.

Finally, there is a small percentage of artists who really benefit from using AI. These are the artists who—even before the availability of AI tools—tended to explore more interesting and original conceptual spaces to begin with. When those artists start using AI to assist them, their work really takes off.

Consistent with the themes of the earlier chapters—particularly the notion of a guiding question—this result tells us about the importance of pointing AI in a promising direction. Instead of giving AI free rein, the most successful artists guide AI toward interesting conceptual regions and then use its rapid-fire abilities to help them "mine" that space.

Research on how people use AI for writing finds something similar. In one study, for example, participants were asked to write a short story. Some were allowed to solicit an idea (or multiple ideas) from GPT to help them come up with a topic. The researchers found that having access to AI increased the quality of people's stories but only when the authors could solicit multiple story ideas and select among them. Going with the first idea AI gives you decreases creativity. Going with the ninety-seventh idea may enhance it.

And for the business world—in what is perhaps the most naturalistic study to date of how professionals are using AI—researchers at MIT asked working professionals to use GPT in their daily work doing whatever is they do best. For example, marketers came up with press releases for a product; HR managers composed a company-wide email; consultants produced a short . . . whatever it is that consultants do. In the end, professionals who were allowed to use GPT completed the task 40% faster. And the quality of their output—as rated by an independent panel of participants—was rated as 20% better. In the hands of skilled professionals of all types, AI was clearly an asset.

Together, this research tells us that the creative benefits of AI depend almost entirely on how we use it. When employed without clear direction—choosing familiar prompts or generic approaches—AI tends to produce boring, homogeneous results. But in the hands of someone who can guide it thoughtfully, AI becomes a powerful tool for expanding creative possibilities.

As AI researcher Dokyun Lee told me, "Creativity consists of both novelty and value. While AI now generates novelty at scale, value remains a human judgment. The most effective creators succeed by leveraging AI's volume to explore widely, then curating with intent."

To return to the archaeology metaphor, think of AI as a powerful excavator. It can rapidly mine creative spaces and generate countless variations. But it needs people to know where to dig and which directions are worth considering. The key is curation: your ability to steer the process, notice promising sparks, and push into new conceptual frontiers.

Surface vs. Deep Work

While systematic exploration can help us discover promising ideas, we've also seen throughout this chapter that many sparks arise in more spontaneous ways—as in the case of Picasso's *Guernica* or Stephen King's *Misery*. Therefore, rather than seeing systematic and spontaneous approaches to Digging as opposing forces, we should view them as complementary: There are times in which our creativity necessitates deep work—periods of focused concentration, systematic trial and error. Then there are other times that call for more surface exploration, where we stay open to unexpected connections and sudden inspiration.

To help navigate this balance, I created the schematic on the next page. This figure highlights the ebb and flow between deep and surface work, showing how, ideally, different stages of the creative process benefit from these different modes of thinking.

The creative process begins with the deep work of Surveying, first with research, building a base of expertise, and identifying where others have found success (*high-resolution Surveying*). Then it's beneficial

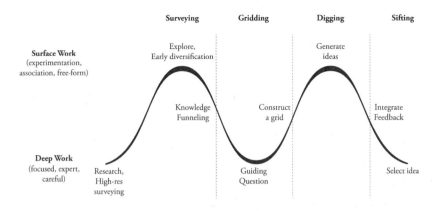

Alternate between surface vs. deep work as you move through the different stages of creative excavation.

to sample broadly and explore. This is the notion of *early diversification*, of being exposed to as many new ideas, social networks, and sources of inspiration as possible. Next you can engage in the process of *knowledge funneling*, carefully reflecting on how those outside ideas relate back to your own expertise.

From this point, you move into the Gridding stage, which requires more focus and precision—especially in the formation of a *guiding question*, which is clearly defining what you are doing and why it matters. From there you can begin constructing a *grid*, which is the process of identifying the constraints of your creative project and using that to help you search that topic area systematically.

Next is the stage of Digging, in which the goal is to unearth as many ideas as possible. Here your idea generation can benefit from more of a "try anything" approach and AI tools. More is more. Remove the guardrails and let the ideas flow freely. But remember that this strategy is most effective when you are mining ideas in the "excavation site" you identified in earlier stages. Digging doesn't mean generating ideas at random—it means trying different angles, perspectives, and approaches within the space you've already mapped out to uncover everything you possibly can from that localized area.

Finally, once you have identified a promising set of ideas, begin to refine. This is the Sifting stage, where you now decide which ideas to pursue further. Like the deep work of the Gridding phase, you want to apply careful scrutiny and deep reflection as you ultimately decide which ideas to keep and which to leave by the wayside. In the final chapters, we will discuss optimal strategies for doing this.

Overall, this figure underscores the notion that you can't approach all aspects of creativity in the same way. Instead, it is essential to change up your approach—alternating between more spontaneous, haphazard exploration to more focused, systematic deep work.

Exercises

Below are several exercises designed to help with Digging for new ideas, with a focus on structured ways of adding small amounts of randomness to your ideation process.

Exercise 26: The Bootleg Tape

Find inspiration from unconventional and unexpected sources.

- **Assemble a "bootleg tape"** of materials that you loosely associate with your project, such as random audio recordings, obscure video clips, or snippets of foreign media. I find that presentation software like PowerPoint or Keynote work best for this.

- **Spend thirty minutes** immersing yourself in this material without any specific goal.

- **Take notes** on anything that sparks an idea or stands out to you as fascinating or unusual.

- **Brainstorm how these elements could be incorporated** into your current project or inspire new directions.

- **Develop at least three concepts** based on your observations and insights from the bootleg material.

Exercise 27: Sensory Overload

Spark creativity by engaging multiple senses, simultaneously.

- **Choose a workspace** where you can control the sensory environment.

- **Prepare a variety of sensory stimuli** (e.g., music, scents, textures, visuals, tastes) that you associate with your project.

- **Spend several minutes experiencing each stimulus** one by one, taking notes on any ideas or emotions they evoke.

- **Then combine two or more stimuli at once** (e.g., playing music and a video at the same time on separate devices) and immerse yourself in this multisensory environment for fifteen minutes.

- **Generate ideas that arise from this sensory overload** and document them.

- **Review your notes and develop** the most compelling ideas further.

Exercise 28: Random Words

Overcome creative blocks by introducing random words and phrases.

- **Use a random-word generator** or flip through a book to select a random word or phrase.

- **Write down the word and think about how it could relate** to your current project.

- **Repeat** this process several times.

- **Identify any new perspectives** or ideas that emerge from this exercise.

- **Try this exercise with a friend and make it a competition**. Who can come up with the better idea relating to the random word or phrase?

DIGGING: THE BIG TAKEAWAYS

The goal in Digging is to get everything out of the ground that you can. Focus on producing a large quantity of ideas. In order to do that effectively you will need to routinely change your approach, your perspective, and your frame of mind. Move beyond mere brainstorming and really think about *mining* the conceptual terrain.

- **Set the Stage:** Allocate dedicated time and space for idea generation. Encourage free-flowing ideas. Beware of the "creative cliff" and push past it. In the end, good ideas are worth waiting for.

- **Search for a Set of Ideas:** Think about finding a set of ideas and experimenting until you find the right combination of elements. When you find an idea you like, pause and come up with several other similar versions. Think about "drilling down."

- **Expand Your Influences:** Engage in early diversification. Experiment with a variety of genres and styles. Similarly, collaborating with weak ties can bring in fresh perspectives that are crucial for creative breakthroughs. When the going gets tough, resist the urge to "turtle up."

PART IV

Sifting

Stories are relics, part of an undiscovered pre-existing world. The writer's job is to use the tools in his or her toolbox to get as much of each one out of the ground intact as possible. Sometimes the fossil you uncover is small; a seashell. Sometimes it's enormous, a Tyrannosaurus Rex with all those gigantic ribs and grinning teeth. Either way, short story or thousand-page whopper of a novel, the techniques of excavation remain basically the same.

—STEPHEN KING, *On Writing*

What does a great idea *feel* like? How do you know when you've struck gold?

Sifting is perhaps one of the most difficult stages of the creative process because, despite conventional wisdom, great ideas aren't always obvious. History is filled with examples where people have stumbled upon a truly transformative idea, completely unaware of its promise. And we are equally likely to make errors in the opposite direction. We may be convinced that we have found something promising when we should have kept searching longer. Like the other stages of the creative process, idea selection is also a highly refined skill that requires patience, careful reflection, and expertise.

This final section of the book unpacks the Sifting stage. In sharp contrast to the optimism of the Digging stage, Sifting requires analysis, critique, and a healthy dose of pessimism. In this section, we'll explore why breakthrough ideas often feel uncomfortable, and how that discomfort, when harnessed properly, can become a powerful motivator. We'll cover strategies for idea selection, such as how to create psychological distance from your ideas, seek input from others, and recognize the right (and wrong) kinds of praise.

Finally, we'll discuss how best to seek feedback and learn from mistakes: What's the best way to pivot while preserving all of the careful work you've done up front? How do you prepare for criticism? Creators and audiences often perceive ideas differently, so we'll explore how to bridge that divide, ask better questions, and anticipate how others will react.

The take-home from this section is that great ideas are all around us. The trick is knowing how to spot them.

10.

Create by Subtracting

It was 1984. Paul Simon's marriage to Carrie Fisher had recently ended, and his previous two albums, *One-Trick Pony* and *Hearts and Bones*, were some of the least commercially successful of his career. The accomplished songwriter was looking for something new, something to jolt him from his funk.

Simon's friend had given him an unmarked cassette of street music from South Africa. The tape became a permanent fixture in Simon's car stereo, and he listened to it nonstop, driving between New York and Connecticut. By the end of the summer, Simon was hooked. He decided that he needed to go to South Africa to find out *who* was making this captivating music.

When Simon got to Johannesburg, he immersed himself in the music community there. He befriended a leading South African record producer who put him in touch with many of the musicians featured on his tape. Simon hit it off with the local musicians and sensed something profound that he needed to unearth in collaboration with those artists.

But there were people close to Simon who cautioned against it. At the time, there were international boycotts against the apartheid in South Africa and questions about cultural appropriation. As Simon recalled, "South Africa is a supercharged subject surrounded with a tremendous emotional velocity. . . . I was following my musical instincts in wanting to work with people whose music I greatly admired. Before going I consulted with Quincy Jones and with Harry Belafonte, who has close ties with the South African musical community. They both encouraged me to make the trip."

Simon booked time at a recording studio and then spent two weeks recording with different local musicians, essentially jamming. At that point, Simon and his collaborators were Digging, generating as much material as possible. As Simon told *The New York Times*,

> My typical style of songwriting in the past [had] been to sit with a guitar and write a song, finish it, go into the studio, book the musicians, lay out the song and the chords, and then try to make a track. . . . With these musicians, I was doing it the other way around. The tracks preceded the songs. We worked improvisationally. While a group was playing in the studio, I would sing melodies and words—anything that fit the scale they were playing in.

After Simon returned to the US, he then spent an entire year editing the material that was recorded in South Africa—selecting engaging segments, piecing them together, overdubbing, and transforming those initial free-form sessions into songs. In fact, the editing was so extensive that Simon and his team were forced to use a newly developed digital audio workstation, pioneering the use of computers in studio recording. The entire album was built from the bottom up, mined from material recorded during those initial live sessions in South Africa.

The result was *Graceland*, an eclectic mix of musical styles and song structures. Simon himself, as well as many of his fans, regard it to be his greatest work.

The making of *Graceland* is a rich example of creative excavation: having a guiding question; transplanting ideas from one genre to another; involving key brokers (like Simon's friend who gave him the tape, or the producer in South Africa); undergoing a lengthy process of exploration and Digging; taking a bottom-up approach allowing ideas to naturally emerge; and finally, engaging in a careful Sifting stage to select and refine what was unearthed.

It is this last step of Sifting, in particular, that I want to focus on. In the hands of a less experienced musician, the same material would have taken a different form. But even among other experienced songwriters, there is something that sets Simon's approach apart. In making *Graceland* and Sifting through troves of previously recorded material, Simon wasn't looking for what he could add—he was looking for what he could *take away*.

Indeed, fascinating research in psychology shows how this keep-only-the-gems approach is in fact much harder than it seems. People often fail to see how subtraction, rather than addition, can be a powerful source of creativity.

To demonstrate this, organizational psychologist Gabrielle Adams and her collaborators at the University of Virginia asked people to edit a wide array of creative work—designs for products, passages of text, and Lego towers. In each case, participants could add, subtract, or alter the work any way they wished. Reliably, however, people tended to "improve" things only by adding more. They hardly ever took away.

For example, in one study, participants received an excerpt of text that contained several redundant sentences and were asked to make the writing better. But rather than remove the redundant sentences, most participants added even more material. Or, in another experiment, participants worked on visual designs. Here, too, participants hardly ever removed visual elements. They just kept adding more.

I've always admired the work of contemporary artist Tara Donovan, who takes everyday household items—plastic cups, toothpicks, masking tape—and assembles them en masse, transforming them into large, atmospheric sculptures that can fill an entire gallery space. I recall once seeing a series of giant, 5-foot cubes Donovan created out of toothpicks and pushpins. The small placard next to the work indicated that the cubes, which were near perfect, were held together only by gravity and friction. I puzzled over how such an object could ever be constructed. Did she precariously add toothpicks one by one?

Then I realized that the artist must have first built a cube frame, filled it with toothpicks, and then removed the frame to reveal the intact cube. This realization was a perfect illustration of how strong our tendency is to look for additions, rather than subtraction.

When revisiting our ideas to refine or improve them, we often think about what we can add. Yet in many cases, the most impactful results come from what we take away.

The Creative Endowment Effect

Why is it so difficult to let go of material? One answer, suggested by the research above, is that subtraction may simply be less likely to occur to us. But a second answer has to do with our attachment to the ideas we generate. In some of my own research on creativity, I've found that we can be reluctant to abandon ideas simply because we are the person who thought of them.

Consider one study in which my collaborator, Jin Kim, and I asked participants to come up with ideas for charitable fundraising. We gave people several minutes to generate as many ideas as they could. Then we asked participants to review their list and select *only* their very best ideas to enter into a competition.

The rules of the competition were that you could submit as many ideas as you wanted, and if those ideas were rated highly by a panel of experts, you would win extra cash for each good idea. The catch, however, was that bad ideas would incur a monetary penalty, meaning that participants were incentivized to submit only their best ideas. To succeed in the task, participants really had to focus on keeping only their top material.

The results surprised us: Not a single participant walked away winning money. The common problem? Participants submitted some very good ideas. But they also submitted several subpar ideas, which erased any of their gains.

Maybe people are just miscalibrated about what a successful idea looks like?

To examine this possibility, we gave a second group of participants the same lists of ideas (generated by the first group) and now told *them* to select only the best ones. The second group fared much better, submitting significantly fewer ideas, and those ideas were, on average, rated as better. This result confirmed something I had long suspected: **Letting go of an idea is harder if we are the person who thought of it.**

This ties into a classic finding from behavioral economics known as the endowment effect—our tendency to value things more simply because they belong to us. This phenomenon can lead to amusing scenarios, such as someone demanding $5 to sell a coffee mug they've just been given, even though they're only willing to pay $4 to buy the same mug from someone else.

Borrowing on this finding, I call our attachment to our own ideas the *creative endowment effect*. We hold on tight to our idea, but if the same idea was suggested by someone else, we would be much more willing to let it go.

We also found—perhaps not surprisingly—that it is quite difficult to de-bias people away from the creative endowment effect. Giving people examples of better ideas, or even explicitly telling them about the phenomenon, does not make them better calibrated. So there is a very real sense in which mere ownership of an idea—the fact that we are the one who came up with it—inflates our perception of its quality.

One remedy for this is simply to pass your ideas off to someone else. Sifting with others appears to encourage greater scrutiny of ideas. It may help us identify points of weakness, see opportunities for subtraction, and reduce the likelihood of missing something great.

A second strategy is waiting. As it turned out, when participants in our studies revisited their own ideas months later, they became significantly more selective. This passage of time allows for psychological distance, making it easier to critically assess one's own ideas.

In keeping with this suggestion, filmmaker and comedian Taika Waititi describes how when he writes a script, he will often write a first draft, put it away for months or longer, reread it, and then rewrite the script again completely from scratch. In writing the second draft, Waititi is able to distill the narrative down to its essence, preserving only what is most central to the core idea.

But getting the input of others or putting projects on pause for months at a time may not always be options. For this reason, it's crucial to develop strategies that help you sift through your ideas in real time. In the remainder of this chapter, I'll introduce several additional approaches and ways of thinking about the Sifting stage that are designed to maximize your ability to let go of subpar ideas while keeping only the gems.

Building a Tower vs. Floating a Raft

I first began thinking about the distinction between "building a tower" versus "floating a raft" in the context of academic talks. When academics present their work to one another, they give a seminar (or "talk") that may last sixty to ninety minutes. The talk usually focuses on a single, narrow topic, and the format is essentially "Here is an interesting topic or question, here's what we did to research it, and here's what we learned."

Often, the talk is composed of a bunch of smaller components, which (in my field) include discussing the results of multiple experiments, reviewing other people's research, and maybe presenting an interesting anecdote or two to illustrate the main point. The questions for would-be presenters: Which content makes the cut for this hour-long talk? Which should I leave by the wayside?

There really is an art to crafting a great talk, which I realize—to nonacademics—may sound a little strange. But a talk that is clear, succinct, and compelling is a very high bar, with potentially huge implications for one's career. Talks are still the primary way in which academic hiring occurs.

To date, I've seen thousands of talks, prepared many myself, and helped colleagues and students prepare a great number as well. And what I have noticed over time is that one of the primary ways in which talks go wrong is in terms of *building a tower*.

Not unlike my two-year-old daughter, who will gather books, blocks, stuffed toys, and perhaps whatever she is eating at the moment to construct the tallest tower she can, before saying "Look, Dada!" when one is giving an academic talk (myself included) there is the impulse to take *everything*—all the studies, ideas, and anecdotes—and try to cram them into the presentation. "Look, here is everything that

My daughter building a tower.

I did! Here is everything that I have thought about and researched regarding this topic."

The problem with this, however, is that your audience is not in the tower business. They are in the raft-inspection business. As audience members, when we evaluate something, we are looking for all the weak spots and holes—the things that will sink the project. Indeed, when we evaluate something, it is almost impossible to silence that inner critic. We want to find the problem areas and identify what's not working to make sure the idea is "watertight."

And that's a *good* thing. A big part of becoming expert in an area is being able to push on arguments and test the internal logic and coherence of an idea.

This insight is not limited to academic talks. Think about a recent movie or work of fiction that failed to deliver. I'd guess that a primary reason why the work came up short was because there were aspects of the story that didn't fit or make sense. Or, in my experience with visual art, the weak spots are often the elements of the work that seem unconnected to the core idea. I've also seen this in business presentations. All the flash in the world cannot compensate for parts of the proposal that seem less thought-out or considered.

So, in trying to "build a tower" rather than "float a raft," you have inevitably included ideas, arguments, or elements that don't necessarily work or fit the main thesis of what you are trying to communicate. And what's perhaps even more interesting is that the very same person—me included—may fail to appreciate that as an audience member, they are in highly analytical raft-inspection mode, whereas when it comes to their own ideas, they are in "building a tower, here's everything I got" mode.

Write Out Your Guiding Question

How do you ensure that you're floating a raft (versus building a tower)? For one, it is helpful simply to be mindful of this distinction. When you are evaluating your idea at the Sifting stage, try to think about floating a raft and identifying all the holes. It's important to remind yourself that the goal is not to showcase everything you've done but instead to present only what's most essential and effective. It is also important to get feedback and to create some distance between yourself and your ideas (as we've discussed already).

But having distance or a critical eye isn't sufficient if we don't know what we're looking for. This is why effective Sifting ultimately comes back to the notion of the guiding question. If you deeply understand and have internalized what you are looking for and why it is important, you can become your most careful and attentive critic, even considering people's natural affinity for their own ideas.

One straightforward way of implementing this is to actually write out your guiding question. Then write a summary of the different elements of your idea and describe their contributions. How does each element add meaning? What problem does it solve? What question does it answer? Now compare what you wrote about your guiding question and what you wrote about your idea. Do all the different elements of your idea serve your guiding question?

This kind of analysis provides a true north and prevents getting derailed from what we are *really* trying to convey. Perhaps you write a beautiful series of lines that are fairly disconnected from your core thesis. It's easy to become enamored by the writing itself, but that can lead you away from the point you were trying to make. The same is also true in visual art, music composition, and several other creative disciplines. Those unnecessary tangents have their own inertia, which can quickly lead to dead ends.

In an interview, comedian David Sedaris offered this helpful advice: "You can sometimes spot that moment where you made a choice that led you to a dead end. . . . Sometimes you'll think, Oh I had that line, and that line was so funny. And then when you try to incorporate that line, you're just building everything around a laugh when you could just go find another laugh."

This advice reminds us that there is an important element of discovery in determining what works. As you follow the breadcrumbs, be wary of the elements that are unrelated to core idea simply because they sound nice or look pretty. Remove the things that don't fit and save them for something else.

Mid-Stakes Events

A second strategy for "embodying the why" and effective Sifting is to set up what I call a *mid-stakes event* in which you present your idea to others.

What is a mid-stakes event? A low-stakes event is one in which you discuss your work in conversations with friends, or colleagues, or your team—which could even be part of the Digging stage. These types of informal conversations are part of the creative process and invariably will lead you to refine your guiding question, generate more ideas, and make new connections. But the reality is that the stakes are not great enough to enforce the type of self-reflective scrutiny and criticism that is needed in the Sifting stage.

At the other end of the spectrum are high-stakes events: a client pitch, a solo art exhibition, a showcase of your material for music producers. High-stakes events are also not the right level to foster effective idea selection. Eventually you will be in the wonderful and enviable position of sharing your creative work with gatekeepers in your industry or the public, but you don't get a lot of these moments in your career. In preparing for those events, you want to be refining and polishing your idea and not still in the process of finding it. Sifting needs to happen before high-stakes events.

A mid-stakes event is something in between a conversation and a super-high-stakes, make-or-break situation. Ideally, it should be a presentation or performance of some kind with a scheduled date. It should have a specific audience. But the potential stakes should not be so great that focusing on the outcome will swallow up any generativity that happens beforehand.

For example, perhaps someone asks you to collect your thoughts for a guest lecture or seminar. If you're a writer, try scheduling a reading of your work to others. If you're an artist, maybe it is a group show. If you're a musician, perhaps it's a gig at a bigger-than-usual venue. If you're in industry, this could be an internal pitch to other departments at your company.

Once you get cued into the idea of a mid-stakes event, you begin to see its potential. It's interesting, for example, how several people who are not necessarily known for public speaking have given college graduation speeches that have gone on to have large cultural impacts: David Foster Wallace's 2005 graduation speech at Kenyon College, "This Is Water"; Steve Jobs's 2005 graduation speech at Stanford; actor Jim Carrey's 2014 speech at Maharishi University commencement, where he offered this advice, "[Y]ou can fail at what you don't want, so you might as well take a chance on doing what you love."

Or consider that Ben Stiller's idea for *Zoolander* originally came from a short spoof to be played during breaks in the 1997 VH1 Fashion Awards. Jack Dorsey pitched the concept for Twitter at podcasting hackathon. Brené Brown's viral breakthrough came from a regional Houston TEDx talk.

There's something about these mid-stakes events—enough pressure to forge great ideas but not too much to stifle them—that can be a wonderful catalyst for creativity. And remember, the value of the mid-stakes event is *not* about the outcome. Rather, it is the effect that preparing for a mid-stakes event has on your creative process.

First, the pressure of an actual deadline will motivate you to dig deeper and pursue lines of thought that you may not have considered otherwise. Second, there is an audience, and chances are that for a mid-stakes event, you will have a pretty good sense of how (at least some of) that audience thinks and responds. As you take an idea from an early, messier form to present it to the outside world, an amazing synergy happens between Digging and Sifting as you start to hone an increasingly clearer picture of what your idea is and who exactly it is for.

Finally, the mid-stakes event will nudge you closer to the "floating a raft" mindset that I discussed earlier, where you are really trying to anticipate the reception of your work through your audience's eyes. Again, the goal of the mid-stakes event is not the effect that it might have on your career, but the work itself. Preparing for the mid-stakes event will push you to discover and develop ideas that you might not have uncovered otherwise.

Look for What You Can Remove

As creators, we must learn to recognize when less is more—when the removal of elements can lead to better results. This approach requires a disciplined eye and seeing beyond the allure of what looks pretty to discern the true value of what's there.

But attachment to our own ideas can blind us to their flaws. Psychological distance becomes invaluable. By stepping back—whether through time or by involving others in the Sifting process—we can see our work with greater objectivity. This detachment allows us to make the tough decisions that are necessary—decisions that often involve letting go of ideas that, while initially compelling, ultimately do not serve the greater vision.

Finally, strategies like writing out your guiding question or preparing for mid-stakes events offer practical means of zeroing in on the method of subtraction. Mid-stakes events, in particular, compel us to confront the gaps in our work, to prune and polish until only the strongest elements remain. These exercises can be an important step in the journey to discover what truly resonates.

Exercises

The goal of these exercises is to boost your ability to sift and get rid of the subpar ideas or elements that just don't fit.

Exercise 29: Overcoming the Creative Endowment Effect

- **Write down a list of all the ideas** you are considering related to your current project.

- **Reach out to a friend or colleague** and give them your list of ideas and ask them to select the ones they think are most promising.

- **Compare your friend's selections** to your favorite ideas. Discuss with them why they chose certain ideas over others. Reflect on any differences in your selections.

- **Time Delay.** After a set period of time (e.g., several weeks or longer), revisit your original list of ideas. Evaluate each idea with fresh eyes.

- **Use the combined insights** from both of these steps to push forward and refine the most promising idea.

Exercise 30: Floating a Raft

Streamline your project to focus on the core idea and remove unnecessary elements.

- **Start by identifying the core idea** or problem your project aims to address. Write a brief statement summarizing the idea.

- **List all the elements** you initially think are necessary for your project. Be exhaustive in this step.

- **Go through your list of elements** and ask, "Does this directly support the core idea?" For each element, consider how it contributes to the main thesis or solution.

- **Begin removing elements** that do not directly support or enhance the core idea. Focus on creating a streamlined version that can "float" without any holes in the logic.

- **Present the stripped-down version** to a mentor or friend. Pay attention to their feedback, especially as it relates to clarity and coherence.

Exercise 31: Grumpy Yoda's Critique

Develop a critical eye for your own ideas by embodying a tough, skeptical mentor.

- **Identify a mentor, friend, or colleague** who is expert in your field and is known for their high standards. This should be someone who you know personally and have interacted with enough to understand their thought process and feedback in a pretty deep way. Just as Yoda was a Jedi expert, you will want to imagine the sage advice of an expert relevant to you and the creative area you are working in.

- **Now the grumpy part.** Imagine this person is reviewing your current project or idea. List all the potential criticisms they might have. Even if the person you are imagining is very warm and encouraging, imagine them in a very grumpy state. They are looking for all the holes they can find in each of your ideas.

Nothing gets by Grumpy Yoda. They see everything—why it works and especially why it doesn't.

- **Try to address each criticism,** not to defend your idea but with an eye to how you can refine and improve your idea as you go. Remember, be tough on the ideas but easy on the person (namely, you). Your goal in Digging was to generate too many ideas, so by definition, there are going to be many ideas or elements that simply don't work.

- **Create a revised version of your idea based** on this imagined feedback and continue refining until you feel the idea can withstand even the toughest (imaginable) scrutiny.

Exercise 32: A Mid-Stakes Event

This exercise helps you design and schedule a mid-stakes event. The goal is to apply the right amount of pressure while maintaining enough flexibility to actually refine your idea or explore new terrain.

- **Identify a suitable event.** This should be a presentation, performance, or demonstration that is somewhere between a low-stakes conversation and a high-stakes, make-or-break moment. The stakes should be significant enough to motivate you, but not so overwhelming that it hinders the creative process.

- **Set a date.** Pick a realistic yet challenging deadline for your event. This is crucial for applying the right amount of time pressure to foster creative progress. Define your audience clearly, keeping in mind that they should be people whose feedback will be valuable, but who are not necessarily gatekeepers for your career.

- **Anticipate audience feedback while preparing and refining.** As you work toward the mid-stakes event, imagine how the audience will respond to your presentation. What parts will resonate with them? What will they find most engaging or valuable? Equally important, think about potential criticisms or questions they may raise. Use these imagined responses to fine-tune your ideas, ensuring you are prepared to address both positive reactions and challenges.

- **Your expectations versus reality.** After your event, carefully attend to a couple of things. First, you want to look at what worked and what didn't. Often that will take some effort on your part to make sure you're seeking feedback in the best way possible—in chapter 12 we will get into the weeds about how best to do this.

Recall that the value of the mid-stakes event is really about the preparation leading up to it. And realizing the full benefits of that preparation depends on how accurate you are in predicting your audience's responses. Therefore, take careful notes about where your predictions were right or wrong. What surprised you? What landed better than you expected? What didn't? This is the real gold to harvest from your mid-stakes event.

11.

How Ideas *Feel*

Following the release of his third studio album, Ed Sheeran teamed up with producers Steve Mac and Johnny McDaid for what was intended to be more of a brainstorming day. It was the first time the trio had worked together.

After they got settled, Mac walked over to the keyboard and began playing a simple melody consisting of just a few chords. Sheeran began strumming and tapping along on his acoustic guitar. The team recorded and looped the two parts and within fifteen minutes, the backbone of a song was in place. An hour later, they had completed the song, with many of the tracks recorded on the very first take. The spark, it seemed, was *there*.

Later that day, Sheeran met with his record label to share the work from the day's recording session. He played the song, but he didn't think it was right for him. Instead, he suggested that Rihanna should perform it. Fortunately, the record label persuaded Sheeran to keep the song for himself. The song was "Shape of You." Not only did it become the most popular song of Sheeran's career, it became one of the most popular songs in recent history.

How did Sheeran almost miss a global hit that was right in front of him? It's not like he was a newbie; he had years of experience with several huge successes under his belt. And Sheeran isn't alone. Screamin' Jay Hawkins forgot that he had even recorded his career-making hit, "I Put a Spell on You." And the rock duo the White Stripes didn't think much of their song "Seven Nation Army" when they recorded it—but if you've been to a sports game or large public gathering (pretty much anywhere in the world), you've heard this tune.

In this chapter we'll explore why sometimes we can be surprisingly bad at recognizing a great idea even after we discovered it. We'll also discuss why at other times we can be too confident or quick to settle with mediocre ideas. Sure, tastes are fickle, and popularity is not synonymous with quality or long-term impact. But the problem is more interesting than that.

A big part of the answer has to do with how it *feels*, psychologically, to have a truly great idea. Often, great ideas can feel unfamiliar and uncomfortable. It's no surprise that the more familiar something is, the more we like it, so almost by definition, a groundbreaking idea will often feel a little weird when it first occurs to us. Our minds are wired to seek comfort in the familiar; therefore, when something disrupts that sense of ease, we instinctively recoil.

But as we'll see, that discomfort can also be an asset—a clue that we are onto something valuable. Feeling uncomfortable with an idea can drive curiosity and lead us toward amazing discoveries. In those moments of doubt lies an opportunity. If we can learn to sit with the discomfort, we might find ourselves on the brink of something transformative.

So then, how do we recognize these moments to then take advantage of them? How do we maximize the Sifting stage to make sure that precious finds are not left by the wayside?

Great Ideas Feel Uncomfortable

In his book *Productive Thinking*, the cognitive scientist Max Wertheimer discusses the discomfort that plagued Einstein while he was developing his Theory of Special Relativity. Wertheimer, who was a friend of Einstein's, describes a series of conversations that the two had in which they talked for hours, alone in Einstein's study. Einstein recalled the train of thought that led him to his hugely transformative theory, and Wertheimer, an astute psychologist, probed him, trying to reach the marrow of Einstein's thinking.

In essence, Einstein had stumbled upon a deep problem concerning how he (and everyone else) had been thinking about the nature of time and motion. Challenging those assumptions felt foreign and uncomfortable—even to Einstein—and Wertheimer's account of their conversations offers a unique glimpse into the process of conceptual exploration that is often glossed over in the historical record and omitted from academic journals.

The plot points of Einstein's thinking were as follows: A young Einstein wonders what it would be like to chase after a beam of light. As an older scholar, he begins to question how a person could ever truly know that they were "at rest" (versus moving alongside everything else). Einstein considers the results of a puzzling physics experiment that gave credence to the thoughts he was having. He asks a question of semantics regarding what it means to say that two events occurred *at the same time*—a thought that plagues him for weeks. Then the resolution, involving the consideration of relativity, an invariant speed of light, and the realization of an intimate relationship between space and time.

Of these facts, Wertheimer has a beautiful insight: "If we were to describe the process in the way of traditional logic, we would state numerous operations, like making abstractions, stating syllogisms, formulating axioms, stating contradictions. . . . But what do we get if we follow such a procedure? We get an aggregate, a concatenation of a large number of operations. Is this aggregate an adequate picture of what happened?"

Wertheimer likens this type of description to wanting to learn about the construction of a building by measuring the location of every brick. The location of each brick tells us about all the stuff involved but nothing about how the construction actually happened. Instead, what we want to know is, why did Einstein move from one thought to the next? How did those thoughts appear? Were they random, simply trial and error?

But then, if they were random, why did they move toward a solution—a solution that upended the core tenets of what was believed at the time? Wertheimer asks, "How did it come about that after he made one step, he followed with just that other step?"

What Wertheimer's questioning implies is that there was a *direction* to Einstein's thinking. If we look at Einstein's reasoning as just a mere collection of thoughts, it is difficult to predict the final destination.

Perhaps, though, it was not the series of questions propelling Einstein forward toward an answer but rather an answer drawing him ever closer with a series of questions. Perhaps Einstein's unconscious mind had a glimpse of a solution—a rough sense of what the final structure should look like. The process of Einstein's creativity then was to close that gap, traversing the conceptual ground between where he was and where another piece of his mind knew he should be.

You may have experienced a version of this in your own creative process: a visual artist who intuitively understands when a particular marking is "right" or "wrong," an author who senses when a phrase sings or doesn't, a musician who knows exactly what the arrangement "needs." Many of us have had the feeling that we are getting *warmer* in our creative process—closer to a successful outcome. And yet when you think about this feeling from the traditional view of creativity—that we are conjuring things out of thin air—it's hard to say what is occurring. If we are simply creating ideas from nothing, how can it be that certain directions in our thought feel more correct than others?

A theory proposed by behavioral economist George Loewenstein helps us understand one piece of this puzzle. Loewenstein's theory says that curiosity is not something purely cognitive—it is more of a visceral state of discomfort or uncertainty. That feeling of uncertainty arises when there is a gap between what we know already and a glimmer of something we want to know but don't yet. Your brain wants to fill in that gap and resolve the uncertainty, which, according to Loewenstein, is what we interpret as curiosity.

Supporting this theory, Loewenstein and his colleagues have found that people are most curious about the answers to questions that they *sort of* know. When we are certain of the answer, curiosity is low. Similarly, curiosity is also low for questions we have absolutely no idea of the answer to. But for questions where we have a vague sense of the answer but aren't entirely certain—questions like "What instrument sounds most like the human voice singing?"—our curiosity for the answer is the highest. (The answer, by the way, is the cello.)

Now let's apply Loewenstein's theory to idea generation. If we're working on a creative problem, like Einstein was, we may also have a vague hunch that there is an answer, *over there*. Then there is the gap in between these two states—between what we know and what we have a glimpse of—which creates a sense of uncertainty. We are motivated to traverse that gap and resolve the uncertainty. In Loewenstein's account, curiosity is an active force that pushes us to seek, to explore further and connect the dots.

The trick is not to abandon this feeling too early. Research by the organizational psychologist Justin Berg has shown that successful ideas can initially feel foreign and abstract. And because of this feeling, creators may discount their full potential or abandon them altogether. The result? Creators often underestimate the promise of some of their most successful ideas precisely because there is this gap in understanding.

When former *New York* magazine editor Adam Moss interviewed visual artist Kara Walker, she described how traversing this gap in understanding had been the secret to creating one of her most famous sculptures. Walker had been commissioned to create an artwork for the old Domino Sugar Refinery in Brooklyn, New York. The empty factory space would soon be converted into high-end condos, but until then, Walker could fill the space with whatever she wished. The task was daunting as the main space alone was over 100,000 square feet.

Walker had been playing with a series of associations—sugar, brown sugar, allusions to Black female sexuality, the slave trade, historical ruins, a sugar refinery explosion she had witnessed as a child. The elements were coalescing, but Walker struggled to connect these different elements.

Then she closed the gap in her curiosity: "Here's what happened: I was on the Q train. And I was reading the Sidney Mintz book [about the history of sugar]. And there's a section where he talks about the subtleties—these special decorative sugar ornaments especially for kings. . . . And I was just like 'Oh, it's a sugar sculpture.' And I realized the Sphinx was the perfect sort of ruin. And that was the big moment." What resulted was *A Subtlety*, an enormous sphinxlike sculpture— 75 feet long and 35 feet high—made entirely of sugar.

Of this, Moss writes, "You'll see that the path that led to *A Subtlety* is a cascading series of associations, but Walker approached it like a research project. I was really surprised at how methodical her thinking was, maybe because some romantic, stubborn part of me believed that artists are all instinct."

Curiosity acts as a powerful catalyst for creativity, bridging the gap between what is known and what is yet to be discovered. Complete ignorance does not fuel creativity, rather it's the tantalizing hint of understanding.

In many instances—science as well as art—the trick is to follow that thread as ideas and associations slowly come into focus until the missing elements are unearthed. But this is easier said than done: The vagueness of abstract ideas and a partial understanding can make us uneasy, which is why the ability to endure uncertainty is so vital. As Einstein and Walker both demonstrate, the key to discovery lies in resisting the urge to shy away from what is uncomfortable and unknown. Instead, lean into it.

Power and Praise Can Be Creativity Killers

Discomfort when ideas are unfamiliar isn't the only feeling that can trip us up—sometimes our positive emotions can too. For example, research by psychologists Angus Hildreth and Cameron Anderson found that when collaborating on creative tasks, feeling more confident in one's abilities can actually backfire and undermine creative success. When people feel powerful, they are more certain that they have the best idea. Instead of listening to others and accepting feedback, individuals who feel powerful talk over others, jockey for position, and spend their time convincing others why their idea is the best.

In contrast, when people are made to feel less powerful, they essentially behave in the exact opposite manner. They engage in more turn-taking, consider ideas from different perspectives, and ultimately wind up selecting better ideas.

And praise can be equally detrimental. When we receive praise for our good works, especially in creative domains, there is the tendency to attribute those successes to deep, personal characteristics, like talent, smarts, or inner genius. While gold stars certainly feel good in the moment, research by Stanford psychologist Carol Dweck suggests that such recognition may have a rather pernicious consequence: If everyone believes we are brilliant, we may be hesitant to prove them wrong. As a result, we are less likely to try new things—dig lots of holes—which is exactly what we should be doing.

In one elegant demonstration, Dweck and her colleagues showed that school-aged children reliably sought out or avoided increasingly difficult problems depending on the type of feedback they received.

After completing a series of puzzles, half of the children were told, "Great job! You must be really smart," while the other half were told, "Great job! You must have worked really hard." Those who were given the "inner genius" feedback were less than half as likely to select harder puzzles in subsequent rounds and were over three times as likely to lie about their performance. Attributing children's success to their inner genius did not psych them up; rather, it led them to take fewer risks and even look for shortcuts. As the saying goes, "If you're thought a genius, better to stay silent than speak and cast doubt."

Our ability to discern more promising ideas is further complicated not only by how ideas feel but also by our beliefs about *who* is likely to arrive at a breakthrough idea. Consider something like artistic genius. When economist Marina Gertsberg and her collaborators analyzed every piece of artwork sold at auction from 2000 to 2017—2.5 million pieces of art produced by more than 100,000 different artists—they found that women accounted for only 4% of the total sales. Only 4%! And, in what I find to be an even more startling statistic, of the top forty highest-selling artists in the sample—the "geniuses"—whose work accounted for nearly half of the total sales (in dollar amounts), there was not a single female artist represented.

The story is the same for museums and galleries. As reported by Gertsberg, female artists represent only 3% to 5% of major museum collections, 30% of artwork sold in commercial US galleries, and only 25% of the work sold at art fairs.

How do we know that the artwork produced by men isn't simply better? A theory in psychology known as the Greater Male Variability Hypothesis argues that whereas men and women don't differ on average in their creative ability, men vary more than women. As a result, there are more men who are at the upper extremes of creative ability. Although the GMVH has minimal support in the creativity literature, the idea is frequently touted as an explanation for why you see a disproportionate number of male creative geniuses.

However, a 2023 meta-analysis of creative performance, conducted in thirty-six different countries, found only a 2% difference in variability across men and women. Moreover, those differences in variability disappeared in more gender-egalitarian countries, suggesting that any observed gender differences in creative performance are more likely due to sociocultural factors. Further, research by Laura Tian finds that although people find men's paintings and women's paintings to be equally skilled when gender is not identified, works *believed* to be created by men are perceived as more skillful and creative. In other contexts, such as business proposals, Devon Proudfoot and her colleagues find that the same business plan is seen as more innovative when it's attributed to a man.

It's impossible to look at these data and not draw an inference about people's psychology. Plainly, when most people think of terms like "genius" or "brilliance" they think of men. What's more, such biases seem to distort people's perceptions about who *can be* a genius, which has other negative consequences.

In research that I conducted with Andrea Vial, Melis Muradoglu, and Andrei Cimpian—psychologists at New York University—we investigated how emphasizing the importance of brilliance in organizations can lead to the systematic underrepresentation of women. Our studies showed that because genius is commonly associated with masculinity, it dissuades individuals, particularly women, from wanting to join organizations who say they value genius or brilliance. We found that instead of communicating that they value intelligence, what organizations really signal when they say they value brilliance is that there is a strong culture of masculinity—that it's bad to show emotions, ask for advice, admit mistakes, or show signs of weakness. As a result, people who don't want to work in a highly masculine environment decide to take their skills elsewhere.

Our Feelings Can Mislead Us

Feelings are complicated. The discomfort you experience when grappling with abstract ideas may be a sign that you're onto something big; it's the gap urging you to push through. But on the flip side, overconfidence and praise can be creativity killers. When you feel too certain, or when others shower you with praise, it's easy to settle for the first good idea rather than pushing toward the great one.

The key to sustained creativity is to embrace discomfort while remaining humble when success tempts you to stop Digging. This balance—between discomfort and confidence—is essential to discovering breakthrough ideas. Below, I've included a few practical strategies for navigating this tension:

Give Every Idea a Shot. When you have an idea, give it the time it needs to develop. Don't rush to discard or embrace it too quickly. Explore its possibilities, sketch out variations, and take it to its logical conclusions. You might discover it's a dead end—but even so, the process often leads to other, better ideas.

Attend to the Awkward Ones. Great ideas often feel strange at first. Instead of dismissing an idea that feels uncomfortable or weird, treat it as an opportunity. Lean into that discomfort, allowing your curiosity to take over. Play with the idea, explore its boundaries, and give your mind permission to wander. Some of your most promising discoveries might initially feel like misfits.

Be Wary of Brilliance. Praise and the label of "genius" can stifle risk-taking. Telling someone they are brilliant may inadvertently reinforce the preference for safe ideas. To keep things simple, focus on the idea itself and how much you like it. If you're in a leadership position, avoid framing your team's creative goals around brilliance or genius, which can exclude diverse perspectives and unintentionally discourage talented people from wanting to join.

Embrace Curiosity, Not Closure. Whether generating ideas by yourself or with others, encourage the habit of asking, "What if?" rather than rushing to find a solution. And don't be afraid to reopen your investigation even if you've already decided to move forward. I find it's often in these later stages of *questioning everything* that I'm able to land on something truly powerful.

Build a Feedback Network. Cultivate a trusted group of people who excel at evaluating ideas on their own merits, separate from the person presenting them. You don't need a large network, just a few individuals who can offer thoughtful, constructive feedback without making it personal. Look for people who consistently challenge your assumptions, not as a way of shutting you down, but as a way of inspiring deeper exploration and uncovering new possibilities.

Exercises

These exercises are designed to help you identify the discomfort that often accompanies new ideas. The trick is to get more comfortable with that feeling, as you use it to your advantage.

Exercise 33: Discomfort into Curiosity

The goal of this exercise is to recognize feelings of discomfort and how that can translate into curiosity.

- **Identify Sources of Discomfort**. Think of some things that make you feel uncomfortable, uneasy, or out of your element. These could be situations, places, or people. They could be certain textures, images, or pairings of concepts. Below are a couple of uncomfortable images to get you started if you are having trouble thinking of something.

- **Reflect on Why They Feel Weird**. For each, reflect on why they make you uncomfortable. What are those feelings of unease? Where do you feel them in your body? What does it bring up in you? Be as descriptive as possible.

- **Find the Curiosity**. For each source of discomfort, brainstorm ways that this feeling could be transformed into a source of inspiration. Ask yourself: What insights can you gain from this feeling? How could leaning into this discomfort push you to think differently? If it is an image, construct a story about what might have happened or why things look this way.

- **Repeat**. Try it again. Tap into the connection between the feeling of discomfort and wanting to know more.

Exercise 34: Embrace the Discomfort

This exercise is about learning to prioritize uncomfortable ideas.

- **Review your list of ideas** that you generated in the Digging phase.

- **Think about how each idea makes you feel**. Does it feel familiar or somewhat uncomfortable or strange? Rank the ideas from most to least comfortable.

- **Focus on the most uncomfortable or abstract idea**. Spend ten to fifteen minutes developing it further. Consider its potential applications, how it could evolve, and what makes it valuable.

- **Discuss this idea with a friend** and pay attention to their initial reactions. Are they put off by the abstractness or unusualness of the idea? What connections do they make?

- **Repeat the process with another uncomfortable idea** from your list.

12.

The Learning Curve

When I was in graduate school, I became mildly obsessed with running. I had been a casual morning jogger, but as my speed and stamina improved, I began to embrace (what were for me) more lofty challenges. Can I run 5 miles? How about 8, or 10? I began to participate in local events, like 5K and 10K runs. Eventually, a goal came into focus: running a 5K in less than twenty minutes—small potatoes for an avid runner, but for me, it was huge. The thought of running a six-ish-minute mile, let alone multiple of them, seemed like an impossibility.

Eventually I got there. I made small improvements in my stride, worked on my pacing, practiced sprinting, lifted weights, and became more serious about stretching and hydration. It wasn't easy, but by remaining focused and making incremental improvements, I achieved my goal.

Around the same time, I decided to abandon art making (though not because of running). As a PhD student, I had the wonderful opportunity to take studio art classes alongside the talented MFA students at Yale's School of Art. As in running, I also wanted to succeed or at least improve in my artistic practice.

But instead of the focused incremental tweaks I made with running, with my art, I shifted wildly between different kinds of ideas and themes. Some things I made were elaborate; others were more minimalist. Some were whimsical, others tried to be lofty and esoteric. At each failed critique, I shifted gears completely only to arrive at an entirely new set of problems.

Why was I able to improve as a runner and not as an artist? There are lots of important differences between running and making art, but in terms of my improvement over time, a key difference came down to this: In running, I was learning. In art, I was merely rolling the dice.

When I set out to improve as a runner, I had a clear goal, and the things I could do to reach it were rather obvious, like fixing my stride or increasing my strength and endurance. In short, I could see what was working and what wasn't and make improvements accordingly. But in art, I didn't really have as clear a sense of what my goal was or how to drill down and refine. When I got feedback, it was hard for me to see what worked and what didn't.

Then there was the identity component. I didn't think of myself as a "runner," so the stakes seemed low. But with art, my identity was wrapped up in it. When each project came up short, I saw it as a reflection on my own artistic brilliance (or lack thereof). Therefore, abandoning and moving in a totally new direction felt more comfortable than sitting down to carefully investigate what wasn't working.

A major theme of this book, however, is that approaching creativity more like running is what increases your chances of success: Take your ego out of it. Have a guiding question. Learn from the success of others. Be a problem finder. Search for ideas in a systematic way. Generate lots of ideas and keep only the gems. Creatives (of all types) find success not by jumping around wildly from thing to thing, but rather by making small, incremental improvements to methodically narrow in.

In the 1930s, an aerospace engineer named Theodore Wright (no relation to the famous Wright brothers) was tasked with estimating the costs of manufacturing airplanes. He observed that in addition to changes in the costs of materials, one of the greatest sources of cost savings comes from learning. For every doubling of the number of airplanes produced, the labor required to build an airplane decreases by roughly 10% to 15%. Said plainly, when people do the same thing again and again, they get better at doing it. We "learn by doing." And if you were to graph that change in cost (or effort) over the number of times you've done something, you would see a downward-sloping curve. Hence the term "learning curve."

This principle, which came to be known as Wright's law, generalizes across a vast number of activities and industries. For example, a research paper that looked at tens of thousands of start-ups found that the most successful entrepreneurs can be readily identified by their adherence to Wright's law.

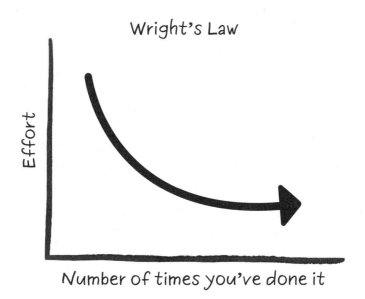

Successful entrepreneurs do not abandon their ideas at each failure, as I did with my art. Rather, they show the characteristic "learning from mistakes" pattern by making slow and incremental improvements. But in order to learn, you have to stick with it. Some aspects of the idea or your creative process need to stay the same, otherwise you are essentially starting from scratch each time.

In this chapter, I'm going to connect several of the themes we've discussed under the umbrella of the learning curve. How could I have made my artistic practice look *more* like running? What were the roadblocks? And how was I potentially getting in my own way?

We'll focus on the power of making slight tweaks to the idea (rather than abandoning ideas completely). We'll discuss the importance of preparing for feedback and listening to different audiences. And we'll discuss how best to prepare for the inevitability of criticism.

The Power of Tweaks

In 1993, the fledgling computer animation company Pixar was anxious to secure a major deal. The company had some critical successes with shorts like *Luxo Jr.*, about a desk lamp come to life, but the awards were not keeping the lights on (so to speak).

Pixar's big break came thanks to a development deal with Disney. The idea was to create a feature-length film made only from computer animation—the first of its kind. In their discussions with Pixar, executives at Disney pushed for making the film "edgier" to help differentiate the Pixar movie from more traditional animated films.

So on the day of the big pitch, Pixar presented the idea for *Toy Story*, a rather sinister tale told from the perspective of a sarcastic ventriloquist's dummy named Woody. Woody was a tyrannical jerk. He threw the other toys around and called them names. The story was dark.

Disney hated it.

The pitch quickly came to be known as the "Black Friday" incident. Not only was the story too edgy, but now Disney had serious doubts about whether computer animation could even work for a full-length feature film. They essentially shut down the entire project.

Ed Catmull, one of the founders of Pixar, describes this moment as nothing short of terrifying. The entire future of his young company was now in question. But rather than abandon the idea completely, the Pixar team pivoted. They landed on a new idea for *Toy Story* as a buddy movie—one that would focus on the relationship between Woody, who was now a warm, charismatic cowboy doll, and Buzz Lightyear, an electronic astronaut action figure. The story was lighter and uplifting. It also allowed the characters to explore complex themes related to aging and feeling irrelevant.

Disney eventually greenlit the project, and *Toy Story* was an instant success. It crushed box office records, won awards, and proved that computer-generated movies could carry a narrative as powerfully, if not more so, than traditional animation.

The development of *Toy Story* underscores a crucial lesson: Often, a minor adjustment or tweak can be enough to transform a struggling idea into a blazing success. In the face of rejection, Pixar could have scrambled to find something totally new. But instead, they listened closely to the feedback, noting specifically what wasn't working while at the same time preserving all of the careful work they had done already. They found a breakthrough success not by starting over completely but by pivoting from the original idea to something adjacent. As Thomas Edison once said, "Many of life's failures are people who did not realize how close they were to success when they gave up."

Interestingly, in his book *Creativity, Inc.*, Edwin Catmull recounts how one of Pixar's star problem solvers, Andrew Stanton, likened this creative approach to archaeology. Stanton was quoted as saying,

You're digging away, and you don't know what dinosaur you're digging for. Then, you reveal a little bit of it. And you may be digging in two different places at once and you think what you have is one thing, but as you go farther and farther, blindly digging, it starts revealing itself. Once you start getting a glimpse of it, you know how better to dig.

Great Feedback Comes from Great Questions

Generating lots of ideas is the secret to finding a few great ones. But this also means that, by definition, many of the ideas we generate will be bad. For example, the mega pop star Dua Lipa wrote ninety-seven songs for her third studio album, *Radical Optimism* (2024)—only eleven made the final cut. Jordan Peele revealed that he wrote and rewrote the script for his award-winning film *Get Out* many times before realizing only he could direct it.

Part of abandoning the "inner genius" view of creativity involves letting go of perfectionism and embracing the fact that much of what we produce (at least initially) won't be good.

The trick then is learning to appreciate what failure can teach you; viewing setbacks as information that helps you further refine and narrow in. After all, learning where good ideas are *not* can be as helpful as learning where they are. Through this lens, rejection provides crucial information to help us identify which version of our idea is most promising. This is what the team at Pixar did when they pivoted from one version of *Toy Story* to another. Or recall how Spencer Silver's repeated rejections at 3M were key to his eventual discovery of Post-it Notes. Through continuous feedback (and rejection), these teams were able to zero in on what worked while ditching what didn't.

What does this look like in practice? Let's return to the running-versus-art example. One important difference, as we just discussed, is making tweaks (like I did with running) versus abandoning the idea altogether (like I did with art). Another important difference has to do with feedback and how we solicit it.

When I was trying to improve my 5K time, I would sometimes run with friends who were experienced runners. If I asked for help, they had no problem telling me what I could improve: "Try making your stride less Frankenstein-like." But art is trickier. Not only does it feel personal, but often the feedback is more holistic, tracking a general liking or disliking. I remember once asking one of my art instructors during a critique, "What makes something good art?" to which he replied, "I guess I know it when I see it." (Perhaps he wasn't seeing it at that moment.)

This means that in lots of creative pursuits, it is on the creator to manage their feedback to ensure they are getting the most out of it. Easier said than done.

Consider a hypothetical situation (which may have actually happened to you): You decide to try a new restaurant. But what initially seemed like an exciting night out turns sour. The decor of the restaurant is a bit off. The music is too loud. After seating you, your server disappears for what seems like an eternity. The food is bland; the bill higher than expected. You decide that while the restaurant may be lovely someday, it is simply too soon—the kinks have not been ironed out.

Then, just as you're about to leave, the manager saunters over and says, "Thank you for dining with us. How was everything?" Before you even have time to systematize all your grievances, out comes "Oh, fine."

Now maybe this hasn't happened to you. Maybe you're the type of person who would let the manager know what you *really* think—and I applaud you. But my point is not about the diner. I'm more interested in the manager and, specifically, how they ask for feedback.

There are certain ways of seeking feedback that are wonderful, that really get to the heart of people's experiences and thoughts. And then there are other ways of soliciting feedback that nine times out of ten are going to get you the "Oh, fine" response, in which you don't learn a darn thing about what people really think.

Feedback is *most* critical when the idea is really struggling. Those are the cases in which the idea benefits most from constructive criticism, and yet these are also some of the most awkward situations to navigate because most of the feedback is negative.

So, what do you do? How do you ask the right questions about your idea?

Purpose of the Feedback. Before you ever seek feedback, first understand what kind of feedback you *really* want. Are you on the fence about whether to even pursue the project further? Are you looking only for positive encouragement? Are there specific aspects that could use a critical eye?

Depending on where you are in a project timeline, some kinds of feedback will be more useful than others. You may be wanting extremely careful and detailed feedback. But at other points, you may just be seeking praise. There's nothing wrong with wanting encouragement or belly scratches—everyone needs them. The key is knowing what kind of feedback you want before you ask for it.

These different goals should change your approach to seeking feedback and also whom you ask. It seems obvious, but if you're mostly looking for encouragement, don't go to someone who tends to be critical. I've certainly made this mistake more than once. Also, try to anticipate what people might say. You know your work better than anyone, so you often have the power to be your most careful and constructive critic.

Provide Context. Once you decide to seek feedback, a bit of context goes a long way. Tell the person about your guiding question. What is your idea and why should it exist? I'm surprised by how frequently people omit this very critical information when seeking feedback. Even if it seems obvious, it can be very helpful for your audience to hear about how you understand your idea and why it is important.

Also, clearly communicate what you are hoping to achieve with the feedback. Your needs will vary at different stages of a project. Let others know the specific areas or questions you need help with.

Ask Better Questions. Instead of asking questions like *"Do you like this idea?"* ask, *"What specific aspects of this idea do you think are strong, and which ones could be improved?"* Ask questions that prompt constructive criticism. For example, *"What is one thing that could make this idea even better?"*

Ask for comparisons to existing ideas. For example, *"Does this remind you of other things you've seen in the past?"* This can be an incredibly straightforward way of understanding how people are perceiving and reacting to your project. (The exercise at the end of this chapter provides additional questions for seeking feedback.)

The point is this: Before you seek feedback, you need to have a plan. You need to understand what you want from it, you need to understand how you will ask for it, and you need to understand what you will do with the feedback once you get it. If you try to respond to every comment from every person, you risk creating more confusion than clarity—not to mention that you are likely to completely zap your motivation. You simply can't listen to everyone.

It is critical then that you try to anticipate different types of reactions and how you will respond, especially if the feedback is negative. What aspects of your idea are you willing to change? Maybe it's nothing. If you are dead set in a particular direction, then feedback may not really be what you're looking for.

The Bell Curve of Feedback

One thing you can count on is that not everyone is going to respond to your idea in the same way. Some people will love your idea, some people may hate it, and many will fall in between. In fact, in most cases, the feedback that you receive will conform to what statisticians call a "normal distribution" (also commonly referred to as a "bell curve" distribution).

Many things in nature tend to follow the bell curve distribution. For example, if you were to select a thousand people at random from the population and measure their height, most people would be of average height (or just around it), while far fewer people would be at the extremes (either very short or very tall).

Chances are that feedback to your idea will also conform to this

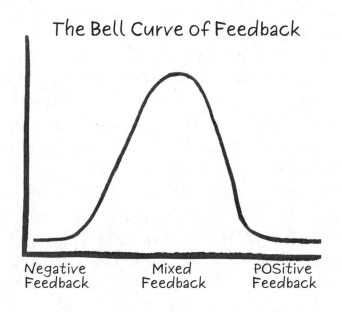

The Bell Curve of Feedback

Negative Feedback   Mixed Feedback   POSitive Feedback

same distribution. A small percentage of people will love it, a small percentage will hate it, and most people will be in the middle—they will appreciate some aspects and not others.

How does the bell curve idea help you effectively plan for and respond to feedback?

First, the bell curve idea interestingly suggests that the feedback we get from most people may not be the most helpful. According to the bell curve idea, most people will be in the middle, but people in the middle may also have some difficulty giving you clear feedback. This may be because they don't have strong opinions, or because they feel some social pressure to curtail their feedback one way or another (think of the restaurant example).

The people with strong opinions, by contrast, have no problem telling you what they like or don't like, so you might get some of the best information from the people on the extremes.

The second way in which the bell curve perspective is useful is that it helps us appreciate that some negative feedback is inevitable. It's like cilantro—many people love it, but some people have a natural aversion. That doesn't make cilantro inherently good or bad; it's simply a matter of taste. Thinking about my ideas this way—like cilantro—removes an element of blame. When people don't like my idea, it's not that I've done something wrong. Rather, some negative reactions are inevitable. The haters were *always* going to be there. This perspective helps me take criticism less personally and focus instead on understanding what those critiques are really telling me.

Third, I think the bell curve idea can be a powerful reminder not to seek feedback too early in the creative process. Given that there are always going to be naysayers, if you are at a point where the project feels a bit tenuous, that may not be the best time to bring in others to see what they think. And remember that even if you fix all the problems people point out, you will still get the same bell curve of reactions—

now the haters will latch on to new things they don't like, or there will be a new group of haters. There's a point where trying to satisfy every critique simply doesn't pay off. Once you've fixed the big issues, it's often better to focus on what's working and make that even stronger.

And finally, the bell curve idea also helps us plan for group feedback. When you move from individual feedback to a group, you're essentially widening the curve. More people means more variance in reactions. A larger group won't just give you more of the same feedback. They'll generate entirely new critiques you hadn't considered before. This can be valuable for seeing your idea from many angles, but it also means you need to prepare yourself for a broader spectrum of reactions. Understanding this in advance helps you approach group feedback sessions strategically, ready to capture this wider range of insights without getting overwhelmed.

So which negative comments should you focus on? Again, this will depend on the specifics of your situation, but as a general rule, the most important issues to address will also probably be what comes up most frequently. This may sound obvious, but I've noticed a curious quirk among creators—we often do the exact opposite. There is a tendency to kind of get numb to the more consistent problems and, ironically, get especially worked up about the one random comment that no one else mentioned.

When multiple people point out the same issue, we often become desensitized to it. It's like background noise that we've learned to tune out. Meanwhile, that one outlier comment—maybe someone who thinks your protagonist should be a talking penguin—somehow gets under your skin and occupies far more mental real estate than it deserves. I think part of this comes from a mistaken belief that common critiques are somehow less important or interesting precisely because they're common. There's also something oddly threatening about a widely shared criticism—it feels more definitively "true" than a one-off comment, which we can more easily dismiss as just one person's opinion.

But that's exactly backward. Common critiques are common for a reason. If multiple people are independently stumbling over the same issue, that's a valuable signal cutting through the noise. While that lone voice suggesting your business book needs more "romance" might be memorable, it's probably not where you should focus your energy.

Think of it like customer feedback for the struggling restaurant. If one person complains that the music is too loud while fifty people mention that the pasta is consistently undercooked, the smart move is obviously to fix the pasta. Yet in our creative work, we sometimes get this backward, obsessing over the music complaint while the pasta problem persists.

To the best of your ability, recalibrate in the other direction. Focus on the negative comments that arise most frequently. If there are common critiques, you will probably get the biggest gains from addressing them.

The Path to Better Ideas

The learning curve teaches us that the greatest breakthroughs do not come from dramatic overhauls but from carefully calibrated tweaks. By testing your work with different audiences, you can piece together what resonates and what doesn't. The trick is to know which criticism to embrace and which to set aside.

Like a sound engineer mixing tracks, you adjust for the right balance, amplifying your strongest ideas and muting what doesn't serve the final product. But this process works best when you approach feedback with a clear plan. Decide in advance what you need—whether it's encouragement, specific critiques, or help identifying blind spots—and tailor your questions accordingly. The more intentional you are about seeking feedback, the more effectively you can narrow in.

When you view feedback as a guide it becomes a powerful tool. Every critique becomes a stepping stone, every failure a clue pointing you closer to success. Great ideas don't arrive fully formed; they're shaped by the steady accumulation of insights and adjustments. Creativity, like running, rewards those who show up consistently and commit to small but meaningful changes.

Exercises

These final exercises are about making feedback work for you. Throughout the book, we've seen that great outcomes come from great preparation. The same is true for feedback. Taking time to plan both how you'll ask for it and how you'll respond will make all the difference.

Exercise 35: Planning for Feedback

This exercise will help you develop a deliberate plan for seeking out feedback, ensuring that you get useful, actionable insights rather than vague reactions.

- **Clarify Your Goal**. Before seeking feedback, think carefully about exactly what you want to achieve. Are you looking to identify weaknesses, validate strengths, or explore new directions? Or are you simply looking for encouragement (which is completely valid)? Being clear up front will help you prioritize the feedback you receive and avoid getting overwhelmed or discouraged.

- **Generate Questions.** The quality of your feedback depends on the quality of your questions. Before seeking feedback, carefully consider what you'll ask. Here are twelve questions to get the ball rolling:

  1. If this were your idea, what's the first thing you'd change? Why?
  2. Is there any part of this idea that you are excited to share with other people? If so, which parts?
  3. If I completely scrapped this and started over, what's the one thing I should keep?
  4. What's the part of this idea that lingers in your mind after hearing it?
  5. If this idea failed spectacularly, what would be the most likely reason?
  6. What's one bold or unexpected direction I haven't considered that might make this better?
  7. If this idea had a tagline, what would it be?
  8. What's the part of this idea that feels the safest? What's the part that feels the riskiest?
  9. What's one thing that feels unnecessary or distracting about this idea?
  10. What do you think my toughest critic would say about this idea?
  11. Who is the perfect audience for this idea? Who would struggle to connect with it?
  12. If I had to simplify this idea dramatically—cut it in half—what should I keep?

- **Prepare for the Bell Curve of Feedback.** Not all feedback is equally useful. Most reactions will fall into one of three categories:

    □ **Positive Reactions:** How will you build on praise? What parts of your idea do you most want to resonate? What will you do if those aspects aren't mentioned?

    □ **Neutral Reactions:** Expect mixed or lukewarm responses—this will likely be most of your feedback.

    □ **Negative Reactions:** What critiques are you willing to address? What elements are you not going to change even if you receive negative feedback? Why?

- **Decide What to Address**

    □ **Summarize Your Feedback:** Write down everything you receive: positive, negative, and mixed.

    □ **Organize by Frequency:** Which comments come up repeatedly? Are there outliers you should ignore?

    □ **Look for Blind Spots:** Are you dismissing certain criticisms because they challenge your assumptions? Are there concerns you anticipated but are hesitant to address?

Exercise 36: Seeing Your Work Through Others' Eyes

The goal of this exercise is to try to imagine that you are someone else who is encountering your work for the first time.

- **Try to vividly imagine that you are someone else.** It is best to imagine you are a person who represents the audience you are targeting with your work. Try to step inside their head, imagine their background, interests, motivations, and what they seek to gain from engaging with your work.

- **Now go through your work and evaluate it as if you were this other person.** How would they interpret it? How would they respond to it? What additional questions might they have?

- **Repeat This Process for Your Creative Hero:** Choose a creative figure you deeply admire and whose work has inspired you. Imagine that you are your creative hero, embodying their mindset, values, and approach to creativity. Visualize yourself sitting in their studio or workspace, reviewing your idea as if it were presented to them.
  - **List at least three strengths** or unique aspects of your idea that your audience member/hero would appreciate or praise.
  - **List at least three criticisms** or areas for improvement that your audience member/hero might point out.
  - **Based on the imagined feedback**, make at least one concrete adjustment to your idea. This could involve changing certain elements, adding new features, or simplifying parts. Write down specific actions you will take to address the comments and enhance the strengths of your idea.

SIFTING: THE BIG TAKEAWAYS

Even the most experienced professionals can miss a great idea lying underfoot, while at the other extreme, we can also become too attached to ideas that we should probably let go of. To improve your accuracy at the Sifting stage, focus on creating psychological distance from your ideas.

- **Beware of the Creative Endowment Effect:** We often overvalue our own ideas simply because we came up with them. Think of your work as "floating a raft" that needs to be watertight, not "building a tower" with everything included.

- **The Power of Discomfort:** Breakthrough ideas can initially feel unfamiliar, abstract, and uncomfortable. But this discomfort can be a clue that you are onto something significant. Allow that tension and curiosity to propel you as you allow these ideas to develop.

- **Learn to Love the Bad Ideas:** Success often involves multiple attempts. Be prepared to refine or even abandon your ideas, recognizing that most of what you generate will probably not be worth pursuing. Seek feedback from multiple sources, but importantly, plan ahead for how you will solicit and integrate that feedback once you receive it.

Conclusion: Getting Unstuck

Creativity isn't magic, nor is it an innate talent reserved for the chosen few. As we've seen throughout this book, creativity is a process of discovery—one that is deliberate, incremental, and available to anyone who's willing to do the work. But like any journey, it's possible to get stuck along the way. Sometimes we hit dead ends, lose the thread, or fail to see the opportunities right in front of us.

In this concluding section, I've outlined some of the most common roadblocks to creative success—and how to break through them.

Roadblock #1: You haven't done enough work up front.

One of the most common pitfalls is jumping into idea generation without laying the necessary groundwork. Many frameworks teach us that creativity starts with brainstorming, but this is an oversimplification.

The real work begins long before you start generating ideas. First, you need to build a foundation, a base of knowledge that helps you understand how others have found success. This comes from defining your *why*. What motivates your project and how will it make an impact? A guiding question—one that is specific, open-ended, motivating, and measurable—helps focus your search. Finally, a systematic approach to exploring a topic, like using a grid, can direct your exploration and ensure that you're considering all possibilities, not just the ones that first spring to mind.

These steps aren't just for beginners. Even experts can benefit from revisiting these fundamentals. If you're encountering failure, it might be because you haven't done the necessary work up front.

Roadblock #2: You've settled on an idea too early.

Another common trap is falling for the belief that "ideas are cheap." While ideas might be abundant, *breakthrough* ideas are rare. Too often, people settle prematurely, thinking they can compensate for a mediocre idea with hard work and polish.

This tendency can lead to narrow thinking and missed opportunities. Many great ideas come from chance encounters and unexpected connections. For example, George de Mestral invented Velcro after noticing burrs stuck to his dog's fur, and the artist Édouard Bénédictus discovered safety glass while experimenting with materials in his studio. Unexpected breakthroughs happen when people are attentive to their environment and open to exploration.

If you've hit a wall, ask yourself: Have I searched widely enough? Have I stayed open to new perspectives and possibilities? Don't settle too soon. Keep Digging until you find an idea that excites you. The right idea will make the rest of your creative journey feel fun and effortless.

Roadblock #3: You've fallen in love with an idea, not the process.

Creativity is romanticized as a flash of brilliance. But in reality, it's often slow and iterative. Great ideas emerge through deep engagement, feedback, and refinement. If you don't love the act of doing—of continually experimenting and pressure testing your ideas—you may struggle to see your project through.

This isn't just about "loving the journey." It's about avoiding over-attachment to any one idea. Our natural inclination is to feel ownership over our creations. Sometimes we push forward with an idea that no longer feels promising simply because of the effort we've already invested. While persistence can be a virtue, it can also blind us to better opportunities. If you've become too attached to your idea—or worse, to the idea of simply finishing your project—it's time to refocus on the process itself.

The Creative Explorer's Toolkit

Overcoming these roadblocks requires a radical shift in thinking. As a starting point, embody the creative explorer. Think about your next great idea as being "out there," as something you will discover. If you're feeling stuck, or confused about where to go next, or wondering how you will ever top your most recent hit, just focus *out*. Take long walks. Visit someplace new. Go to the library and choose a book at random. Try to expose yourself to as much new information as possible, from as many different sources as you can.

Don't be an Originality Ostrich. Remember, the spark of creativity comes from what's new to you, not what's new to everyone. If you're feeling stuck, begin by emulating something familiar, tweaking it, and gradually making it your own. Great ideas often start as a slow crawl from the familiar into the unknown. And disregard the comment *"it's been done before"*—that phrase is a creativity killer. You will inevitably put your own spin on things. The existence of similar ideas simply means that you're exploring fertile ground.

Expand Your Influences. Creativity flourishes when we engage with people and ideas outside our immediate expertise. By expanding your network and exposing yourself to different perspectives, you create fertile ground for connections that might not otherwise occur. This process of diversification can be especially powerful early in your journey, as it helps uncover concepts and skills that will ultimately enhance your work.

Be a Problem Finder. Another critical piece of the puzzle is becoming a problem finder. Look for gaps, hidden questions, and the negative spaces that others miss. Try to let go of your preconceived notions and your "inner explainer." Blazing-hot ideas may be right in front of you, waiting to be noticed.

Embrace the Constraints. Limitations, barriers, "boxes"—they don't hinder your creativity. In fact, they are the engines propelling your idea forward. Not only are constraints something to react against; they also give us a powerful framework for thinking systematically about a project. As a result, don't avoid the constraints, run to them. Limit your artistic palette, compose a musical piece on a kazoo, decrease your budget, impose more limitations. The more rigid your box, the better you will think *within* it.

Keep Digging. When brainstorming, we often think that we're about to run out of ideas or that we've exhausted the conceptual terrain. But that is an illusion. Whatever your allotted time for brainstorming, or however many ideas you think you *can* come up with, double or even triple that number. Keep going. You will not run out of ideas, and in fact, the point at which you think you are about to exhaust every idea you can possibly come with—that's probably when things are first starting to heat up.

Explore the Uncomfortable Ideas. Of course, not all great ideas feel "great" in their early stages. Some might seem strange, abstract, or even uncomfortable. These are often the ideas worth pursuing. The discomfort is a signal that you're venturing into new territory, exploring concepts that others might have missed. Give those uncomfortable ideas time to take shape and heat up. You may be surprised at what they become.

Think about Floating a Raft (versus Building a Tower). When it comes time to refine, remember that your audience will care more about how your idea fits together than how much effort you've invested. This is the moment to ensure your idea is watertight, like a raft, rather than a towering structure built up with unnecessary details. Be ruthless about removing pieces that don't fit. Save them for another project if you must, but don't let them sink your idea.

Invite Others In. Creativity thrives when you invite others into the process. Other people bring fresh perspectives, spark new ideas, and reveal blind spots you might have missed. Whether it's a structured "mid-stakes" event like a presentation or something more informal, collaboration offers an invaluable opportunity to refine your thinking. The act of creation itself is deeply personal. But involving others at the right moments can elevate your ideas in powerful and unexpected ways.

Ideas Are All Around You

You are now a creative explorer, equipped with the necessary tools to discover what's already there. But great ideas don't exist in some distant, elusive realm. They are right in front of you, embedded in everyday experiences and perhaps disguised as mundane or commonplace. The challenge is to see the untapped potential all around you, to keep Digging when others might stop, and to embrace the iterative nature of discovery.

Take the unexpected case of cascatelli. Dan Pashman—host of *The Sporkful* podcast—spent years obsessing over something that most of us take for granted: pasta. He had a vision for the perfect pasta that would hold sauce better, sit well on a fork, and offer a satisfying bite. After countless iterations, expert feedback, and a lot of trial and error, he finally arrived at cascatelli—a new pasta shape resembling a wavy rainbow that not only fulfilled his vision but also took the food world by storm.

The beauty of this example is that it shows innovation in one of the oldest, most saturated domains. Pasta has been around for millennia, and yet there was still room for something new. What's more, the innovation wasn't radical. It was incremental. Cascatelli was born not out of completely rethinking pasta, but from iterating on an existing idea. Pashman saw what wasn't working in other kinds of pasta and used those observations to create something better.

Now it's your turn. Where do you see opportunities to dig deeper? What assumptions can you challenge? What habits can you build today to unearth your next great idea?

My hope is that this book has given you a new outlook on what creativity is and where great ideas come from. The truth is that we're all capable of finding something. The key is knowing where to look, how to search, and what to do once you've found it. Keep Digging. Your next creative breakthrough could be closer than you think.

Appendix:
Deeper Questions About
Creativity

In discussing this book with friends and colleagues, certain questions came up again and again. Some questions were about the fundamental nature of creativity, while others concerned more practical implications. This appendix addresses these recurring questions, from the basic *"What is creativity?"* to more nuanced questions about implementation and value. My hope is that this section not only clarifies potential misunderstandings but also deepens our exploration of how creativity works and how we might better foster it.

What is creativity?

In the academic literature, creativity is typically defined as the process that leads to new and useful ideas. But why these two components—new *and* useful?

The "new" part is relatively uncontroversial. Nearly all dictionary definitions of creativity highlight novelty, and research consistently shows that people associate creativity with originality. If an idea is not new in some way, can we really call it creative?

But what about useful? Useful in this context does not merely mean functional, like a tool. Rather, it refers to some form of value or impact—or, as it's called in some disciplines, utility. In business or technology, creative ideas meet people's needs in a novel way. In science, creativity reveals new ways of explaining our world, which in turn allow us to solve problems, make predictions, or satisfy our curiosity. In art, literature, and music, creativity is more about creating meaning, evoking emotions, or offering a new way of seeing. Many types of creativity may be intended simply to capture our attention and entertain us.

These different forms of value—whether emotional, intellectual, or social—make creative work useful in ways that transcend mere functionality.

In chapter 2, I referenced a *Simpsons* episode where Homer becomes an inventor, creating things like the Everything's Okay Alarm and the Makeup Shotgun. Are they new? Absolutely. But they fail to meet any real need. The joke, of course, is that Homer sees them as brilliant innovations, while everyone else sees them as useless or even harmful. That's the tension: Creativity depends not only on what's new but also on how the idea impacts its audience.

Therefore, new and useful are not simply two separate elements of "creative" ideas—they are deeply interconnected. What makes an idea *creative* is that it *offers a new source of value*: a new solution to a problem, a new way of seeing something, a new way of evoking emotion. The way in which a creative idea needs to be new is in terms of the value that it provides.

Art is a fascinating case because it stretches the idea of usefulness in unexpected ways. Consider Maurizio Cattelan's artwork *Comedian*—a banana duct-taped to a wall, which sold for $6 million. The object is not useful in any traditional sense. But within the world of contemporary art, the piece has value—not as a tool, or home furnishing, or food, but as a statement. Is it a critique of the art market? A commentary on meaning-making? A stunt? Maybe all three. Either way, it provoked conversation, which suggests that in its own way, it did something. It had an effect.

But does that make it creative? That depends on whom you ask. The same idea can be seen as groundbreaking in one context and irrelevant in another—useful by some and useless by others. That's why creativity is hard to pin down. It isn't just about a single person generating an idea but also about how that idea is received. Some ideas spark immediate recognition, while others gain appreciation over time. Some are valued only within a niche community, while others reshape entire fields.

In this sense, creativity is part of an ongoing discussion about meaning, deciding what matters, and which ideas are worth carrying forward. And determining what matters isn't static. It shifts as cultures evolve and different audiences reinterpret.

If we take this view that creativity is about realizing new sources of value, then creativity also isn't unique to humans (and I don't mean elephants that paint). I mean the kind of innovation we see in nature, where other species discover new ways of solving problems of survival—like orcas developing distinct hunting techniques, or chimps fashioning tools to access food. Is the idea for fast-food delivery fundamentally different than the idea to use a frayed stick to harvest termites from a mound? Both are new solutions to get food faster and more efficiently. Even a beaver's dam is, in a sense, a creative object. It alters the environment in a way that benefits the beaver, much like humans reshape the world through architecture, technology, and language.

In sum, creative ideas are "creative" because they bring new sources of value to people. That said, what makes something valuable (or useful) is a shifting target. It varies by the type of work in question and who is evaluating it. It is part of a larger conversation. Perhaps, then, the most interesting question isn't "What is creativity?" but rather "Where does the capacity to create come from?"

Are new sources of value (however they might be defined) entities that arise from within us, or are they part of the external world?

What do you mean by the notion that ideas are external to us?

Over millions of years, we humans evolved specific cognitive tools for perceiving and understanding our world. You can think of the collection of these cognitive tools as an operating system of sorts, "Human N.0." Our operating system does an immense number of things: It takes a wild cacophony of sensory information and converts that raw data into meaningful shapes and sounds. It provides the architecture for language. It makes sense of other people's faces and emotions, telling us when someone is elated, or sad, or angry. It allows us to remember the locations of food sources and predators, and assigns values to those outcomes, helping us seek out things that keep us alive and avoid what doesn't.

Importantly, however, Human N.0 is not a perfect reflection of reality. Rather, it is nature's best attempt to develop solutions that work for us—our unique biology and mental hardware. As the philosopher Alfred North Whitehead reminds us, the vivid Technicolor we associate with the external world is, in fact, something we, over millions of years, have developed—not something that we directly perceive.

Thus, nature gets credit which should in truth be reserved for ourselves; the rose for its scent, the nightingale for its song, and the sun for its radiance. The poets are entirely mistaken. They should address the lyrics themselves, and should turn them into odes of self-congratulation on the excellency of the human mind. Nature is a dull affair, soundless, scentless, colourless; merely the hurrying of material, endless and meaningless.

This discrepancy between how we perceive the world and how it actually is can be readily experienced in visual illusions. For instance, look at the image below. Most people, when they stare directly at the image, perceive that the heart is growing and expanding. You can't help it. Even though part of you knows that the heart cannot be changing size, the way your operating system is "programmed" makes the illusion irresistible.

Visual illusions reveal the places where our operating system and what's *really* there diverge. We know that the heart isn't moving—it can't—but our operating system tells us that it is.

How do we understand this illusion in the universe of ideas? And I don't mean the explanation of why the illusion occurs, but the image itself. Where does the idea for this particular illusion *live*? Is it something that someone created? Did it just spring forth from someone's

Copyright © Gianni A. Sarcone, giannisarcone.com, all rights reserved.

head, popping into existence? Or should we think about it more as a discovery?

Well, in one sense, the Expanding Heart illusion was clearly created. A wonderful team of researchers in Italy, who run a nonprofit called the Archimedes lab, developed it in 2013. They entered it into the Best Illusion of the Year Contest (yes, that's a real thing) and it almost won. No one had seen this image before 2013, and now you're looking at it here.

But there's another sense in which the Expanding Heart illusion is more like a discovery. Because of how our brains our wired, we were always going to perceive this collection of ink in this way. And now that we know that this kind of illusion exists, you can take silhouettes of other kinds of objects, plop them in the center, and get the same effect. The principles that give rise to this illusion existed long before 2013, and long before there was ink or paper. It is a product of how all our minds evolved to perceive the world.

In this sense, developing the Expanding Heart illusion was a discovery. It was about arriving at a particular location in conceptual space.

As another example of this same idea, consider the Library of Babel, a fascinating project created by an author-programmer–literary theorist named Jonathan Basile. The Library of Babel (based on Jorge Luis Borges's short story) is an online repository that, according to its website, contains "every book that ever has been written, and every book that ever could be—including every play, every song, every scientific paper, every legal decision, every constitution, every piece of scripture, and so on. At present it contains all possible pages of 3,200 characters, about 10^{4677} books. . . . Every possible permutation of letters is accessible at this very moment in one of the library's books, only awaiting its discovery."

Out of curiosity I searched for the text that directly precedes the paragraph about the Library of Babel, beginning with "But there is another sense" and ending with "arriving at a particular location in conceptual space." Indeed, that identical paragraph appears word-for-word in its entirety in the Library of Babel—it has been "written" already. In fact, it appears roughly 100,000,000,000,000,000,000, 000,000,000 times.

We can think of visual illusions, prose, and by extension, a nearly infinite number of other ideas as existing in space that is neither the external real world nor something that is purely in our own heads. Rather, we can think of ideas as existing in an abstract realm known as the *conceptual landscape*—a vast terrain where the connections between different ideas and their complex interdependencies shape the overall topography. This landscape is the product of our operating system. It comes from all the different elements of Human N.0 running wild and interacting as they bump up against reality.

This notion of a conceptual landscape is actually a very old idea. Over two thousand years ago, Plato introduced the idea of universal forms that transcend the physical world. In the 1900s, Lev Vygotsky, a pioneering developmental psychologist, used this idea to understand how despite wildly varied childhood experiences, children seem to acquire the same cognitive appreciations at similar times. And the idea of a conceptual landscape is used today by cognitive scientists like Margaret Boden, who has written extensively on the topic; network scientists, who research complex systems; and more recently, computer scientists exploring the frontiers of generative artificial intelligence.

The conceptual landscape gives us a way to talk about a universe of ideas independent of the people who think them. Some of the ideas that live in the conceptual landscape have been discovered already, but a great many are lying dormant, waiting to be unlocked.

What do you mean by the term *resonance*?

The ideas that reside in the conceptual landscape are ultimately grounded in reality. And this means that there is a hierarchy among them. Some ideas are better reflections of reality than others. Or more precisely, some ideas are better adaptations to reality *for us*. They are more useful. They bring us more pleasure or joy. They allow us to do things we couldn't do before like land a spacecraft on the moon.

I use the term *resonance* to characterize this idea. Resonance describes a point of fit—a solution—between how we understand the world and some deeper truth about how the world actually is.

Suppose, for example, you lived in a small village next to a waterfall. Living near the waterfall, you would come to notice the energy realized by the falling water. Eventually, you may have the idea of harnessing some of that energy to help accomplish your daily tasks, like milling flour or grinding wood into pulp. Given the basic principles of physics and engineering, chances are that your device would contain elements that are common to most water mills—a waterwheel, paddles, axle, gears, etc. And your water mill would probably be very similar in design to other water mills all over the world, even if your village was completely isolated. In this way, we can think about the idea for water mills and their basic design as a point of resonance. Various environmental and engineering constraints will give rise to the same successful solution again and again.

Which is not to say that there is only one design for a water mill, or that it's impossible for improvements to be made—think hydroelectric dams. Instead, my point is that there is a need for humans to harness the power of the falling water. There are also certain characteristics of waterfalls, certain characteristics of various building materials, basic principles of engineering, and so on. A point of resonance reflects how the amalgamation of all that physical *stuff* comes together to satisfy the underlying need, to varying degrees.

Similarly, scientific ideas like Einstein's Theory of Special Relativity reflect another type of resonance. In this case, the idea satisfies a point of fit between the laws that govern the universe and the abstract systems we have devised to understand those laws (physics and mathematics). Indeed, we can think of creativity in lots of different domains as the search for—and the discovery of—different points of resonance. The bicycle is a point of resonance for how to move around using your own power. The telephone is a point of resonance for how to communicate over long distances. The sandwich is a delicious point of resonance for how to eat on the go.

Finding a point of resonance does not mean that we need to understand fully why the solution works. For example, it may surprise you to learn that even though bicycles have existed since the early 1800s, even today scientists do not know why it is possible to steer a bicycle merely by shifting one's weight. Indeed, as we have seen in this book, there are many instances throughout history in which the solution precedes the problem—where someone discovered a point of resonance well before the uses of that point of resonance are known. Many great ideas arrive in the form of answers searching for questions.

If creativity involves a process that is external to us, does the individual matter at all?

Yes. A big theme of this book is that creativity has a method. There is a process to discovering new and useful ideas. Therefore, creativity can be improved by adopting specific approaches and engaging in focused practice. Like with anything, some people may have a head start or find acquiring the skill easier than others. But ultimately, the data suggest that *how* a person approaches creativity is a lot more important than *who* the person is. The entire book has been about this thesis, so I won't rehash specific points here.

At the same time, there are also larger forces involved—forces that extend beyond the actions of any one individual. Consider the invention of the snowmobile, often credited to Joseph-Armand Bombardier. At the age of fifteen, Bombardier built a prototype for a snow-traversing vehicle using an old engine and some sleds. He moved on to other ideas and several years passed. But in 1934 tragedy struck. Bombardier, his wife, and their two-year-old son lived in the remote town of Valcourt, Quebec. In the midst of the harsh Canadian winter, Bombardier's son fell ill with peritonitis (a severe inflammation of the abdomen). The deep snow proved impassable and, sadly, the boy died before the family could reach the hospital.

Determined to prevent similar events from happening again, Bombardier set to work perfecting the snow-traversing vehicle he had designed as a boy. By essentially fitting an automobile engine to a sleigh, replacing the wheels with a track system, and adding a ski system at the front for steering, Bombardier created the first snowmobile. A few years later, he had completed the design and patented it.

The invention of the snowmobile wasn't about creating something entirely new, but rather combining existing technologies in a novel way. However, without the prior existence of the automobile engine, a track system, and a steering mechanism, Bombardier would have needed to re-create each of those components from scratch, retracing centuries of development and refinement.

This notion, that new ideas and innovations build upon existing ideas, is known as the *adjacent possible*. It is a term coined by a biologist and physician named Stuart Kaufmann (and later popularized in a wonderful book by Steven Johnson, *Where Good Ideas Come From*).

In essence, the adjacent possible says that what becomes possible or "thinkable" in the future depends on what exists now. And what exists now is a result of what existed before.

Imagine a marble rolling down a mountainside shaped with ridges and valleys. The farther it descends into a valley, the more entrenched it becomes. So too, in the realm of ideas, the concepts we arrive at are products of what's around us, what came before us, and what other people are doing. There is an energetic flow—a cascade—to the discovery of ideas, such that the ideas available at one moment in time constrain the range of ideas that may emerge later. In the case of the snowmobile, because of the existence of *adjacent* technologies— automobile engines, a track system, skis—it wasn't until the 1930s that the snowmobile was even *possible.*

As a result, there is a sense in which that particular time—the early 1930s—was ripe for the snowmobile's invention. Of course, it's possible that if not for the tragic loss of Bombardier's son, the idea for the snowmobile might have lain dormant for another few years. But then we can also imagine someone—not Bombardier—who was similarly talented and motivated, looking at the available technologies of the day and devising their own version of the snowmobile.

And in fact, that's exactly what happened. As another example of multiple discovery (discussed in chapter 1), there were actually two other people, working completely independently from Bombardier, who had the very same idea at roughly the same time: A man named Carl Eliason in Wisconsin patented a design for the motorized toboggan in 1927, and in the 1920s, Virgil White from New Hampshire began selling snowshoes for automobiles—essentially skis that could be fitted to the front of a Ford Model T.

Many great ideas come from improvisation or mistakes. How does this fit with your theory?

Great ideas frequently come from improvisation and mistakes, which is entirely compatible with my view of creativity. First, when we are talking about successful mistakes or improvisation, we are often talking about individuals who have significant expertise. In the language of this book, they have Surveyed the conceptual terrain and know what successful ideas look like in their area.

Second, those individuals often have a guiding question. Their question does not need to be explicit. But for a comedian working on their routine or an improvisational musician, they have already focused their "compass" by having an understanding of what they are looking for and the constraints involved. So, in terms of Gridding, there is also mastery.

From this perspective, what is happening when people improvise or make a fortuitous mistake is that they are engaging in a form of Digging. The free-form exploration, or happenstance, or misunderstanding has led them to unearth some niche area of the excavation site. In this sense, mistakes and accidents are simply another kind of idea generation.

And finally, in terms of Sifting, the same expertise is also important. A musician has to be expert enough to realize when improvisation has yielded something important. An inventor has to realize when a fluke might actually have potential. I would guess that for every mistake that has yielded a great idea, there are hundreds of potentially successful mistakes that went unnoticed precisely because the person who stumbled onto the idea lacked the relevant expertise to identify it as promising in the first place.

Are you saying we should just throw a bunch of things at the wall and see what sticks?

No. In my view, unguided search, unaided by knowledge or a deeper understanding of what leads to success, is unlikely to result in much of anything at all. That said, we tend to underestimate just how much search it takes to find successful ideas and just how many iterations are needed. As a result, we tend to settle for ideas too early. Also, I think many people discount the importance of randomness and exposure to new sources of input and stimulation.

Are you saying that how well an idea is executed or implemented doesn't matter?

No. Execution and seeing a project through are essential. But we often give too little credit to ideas themselves and to how impactful even the smallest kernel of a good idea can be. I've tried to tackle some of the dynamics that pertain to implementation. That said, most of this book is focused on the question of how we arrive at ideas, rather than what to do once we've chosen the right one to develop.

The world is already flooded with many subpar ideas— are you suggesting that people generate even more?

No. I strongly support criticism, editing, and curation. However, it is important not to confuse the final product for the process.

Statistician and design guru Edward Tufte proposed the compelling idea that when conveying information, we should strive to maximize a data-to-ink ratio. In short, communicate as much information as you can with as little ink as possible. Simplify. This same principle holds true in most domains. There is something inherently beautiful about a minimalist painting, a perfectly crafted sentence, or a sparse but evocative musical recording.

But when we approach idea generation, don't confuse the final product for the process. It is noble to try to maximize something like a data-to-ink ratio in the end, but that is different from the amount of ink we often need to spill beforehand (hint: It's a lot!). In other words, the "less is more" mantra has a certain appeal for how we may evaluate the final thing once it's polished and presented, but in many creative endeavors, it dramatically misstates the process of getting there. As the philosopher Edmund Burke famously put it, "Expense, and great expense, may be an essential part in true economy."

Generate many ideas but then be selective (ruthless even) about which ones actually get developed and put into the world.

Don't phrases like "good idea" or "great idea" assume some value metric? Isn't determining what's good ultimately subjective?

Yes. In writing this book, reviewing the scientific literature, and conducting studies of my own, I've made certain assumptions. And undoubtably, those assumptions may have flaws, as there is inherent subjectivity in determining what is good or important. To quote one of my favorite films, *The Breakfast Club*, in which Brian, a straight-A student, is aghast that he failed shop class: "Did you know without trigonometry, there'd be no engineering?" Brian asks. To which the deadbeat Bender replies, "Without lamps, there'd be no light." The point is that all our efforts and contributions matter.

That said, there are times in life when we have to produce *something*. And that something will ultimately be evaluated in some way. And if want to try to figure out what approaches to creativity make some things better received than other things, we need to have some way of talking about them and comparing them.

In the book, the two metrics that I have discussed most often are impact (i.e., how many people gravitate toward the idea or in some way adopt it) and disruption (i.e., the extent to which the idea affects or changes the status quo). This does not mean that these metrics are free from cultural specificity and bias. Nor does it mean that all successful ideas are recognized as such in their time—many are not.

Ultimately, the true judge of what's good is you. That may be the only metric that really matters. My hope is that some of the ways of thinking in this book lead to ideas *you* feel are worth pursuing.

Acknowledgments

It would be ironic for a book about discovering ideas to ignore the many external sources that shaped it. In some form, every idea in this book is drawn from somewhere.

First, I'd like to thank the many researchers and theorists who have influenced my view of creativity. If you're not familiar with their work, I encourage you to seek them out: Teresa Amabile, Justin Berg, Mihaly Csikszentmihalyi, Malcolm Gladwell, Adam Grant, Douglas Hofstadter, Steven Johnson, Austin Kleon, Dokyun Lee, Dean Simonton, Twyla Tharp, Brian Uzzi, Rob Walker, and Dashun Wang.

Second, I'm deeply grateful to my collaborator, Jin Kim; to Joshua Knobe, Frank Keil, Paul Bloom, Gal Zauberman, and Justin Junge for their thoughtful comments on different stages of the project. To my agent, Alison MacKeen, and to Alexis Burgess for essential early input that helped shape the book and give it structure; and to my editor, Stephanie Frerich, as well as editorial assistants Tzipora Chein and Brittany Adams, for their skilled and steady guidance throughout.

Finally, I'm forever grateful to my mother, Nancy; brother, Rob; and my late father, Lou, whose support has meant the world to me.

And most of all, to my wife, Rachel, and daughter, Loa:

Rachel—for being my lifeline of encouragement and forward momentum; for reading multiple drafts and offering deep, incisive comments; and for being a wellspring of ideas and generative connections that profoundly changed this book for the better.

And to Loa—for being a constant reminder that we come into this world as curious, wide-eyed explorers—and that perhaps our most authentic mode of being, as creatives or otherwise, is returning to that state.

Notes

Part I: Surveying

7 *"My so-called inventions"*: "Thomas Edison's Greatest Invention," Derek Thompson, *The Atlantic*, October 22, 2019.

9 *"I thought we were"*: "Fossil Finders: Kamoya Kimeu Carol Broderick," *The Leakey Foundation Newsletter*, April 13, 2018, https://leakeyfoundation.org/fossil-finders-kam oya-kimeu/.

9 *"To some of our visitors"*: "Fossil Finders," *Leakey Foundation Newsletter*.

9 *"Within ten minutes"*: Virginia Morell, *Ancestral Passions: The Leakey Family and the Quest for Humankind's Beginnings* (New York: Simon & Schuster, 2011), 262, 526.

10 *Kimeu is personally responsible*: Clay Risen, "Kamoya Kimeu, Fossil-Hunting 'Legend' in East Africa, Is Dead," *New York Times*, August 11, 2022.

Chapter 1. Burn the Cabin Down

13 *"Writing is easy"*: Randolph Hogan, "Book Ends: Writers on Writing," *New York Times*, August 10, 1980, BR9.

15 *The reality, however*: "Myths and Misconceptions," Walden Woods Project, https://www .walden.org/education/for-students/myths-and-misconceptions/.

15 *Consider a fascinating study*: Mathias Benedek, Gülcihan Yaren Calisgan, and Janika Saretzki, "How Do Creative Professionals Stand Out? Comparing the Creative Potential of Musicians and Actors to Non-artists," *Personality and Individual Differences* 236 (2025): 112993.

17 *"the greatest living painter"*: Derek Thompson, "Hot Streaks in Your Career Don't Happen by Accident," *The Atlantic*, November 1, 2021.

17 *When the research team*: Lu Liu, Yang Wang, Roberta Sinatra, C. Lee Giles, Chaoming Song, and Dashun Wang, "Hot Streaks in Artistic, Cultural, and Scientific Careers," *Nature* 559, no. 7714 (2018): 396–399.

18 *When the Northwestern researchers*: Lu Liu, Nima Dehmamy, Jillian Chown, C. Lee Giles, and Dashun Wang, "Understanding the Onset of Hot Streaks Across Artistic, Cultural, and Scientific Careers," *Nature Communications* 12, no. 1 (2021): 5392.

19 *conform to a complex repeating pattern*: Richard P. Taylor, Adam P. Micolich, and David Jonas, "Fractal Analysis of Pollock's Drip Paintings," *Nature* 399, no. 6735 (1999): 422.

19 *This led Taylor and his colleagues to speculate*: Richard P. Taylor, Branka Spehar, Paul Van Donkelaar, and Caroline M. Hagerhall, "Perceptual and Physiological Responses to Jackson Pollock's Fractals," *Frontiers in Human Neuroscience* 5 (2011): 60.

19 *identified a similar tree-branching pattern*: Gert J. Van Tonder, Michael J. Lyons, and Yoshimichi Ejima, "Visual Structure of a Japanese Zen Garden," *Nature* 419, no. 6905 (2002): 359–360.

20 *Multiple discovery was first documented*: William F. Ogburn and Dorothy Thomas, "Are Inventions Inevitable? A Note on Social Evolution," *Political Science Quarterly* 37, no. 1 (1922): 83–98.

22 *"In the few circumstances"*: Mark A. Lemley, "The Myth of the Sole Inventor," *Michigan Law Review* 110 (2011): 709.

22 *There is a sense*: Malcom Gladwell, "In the Air," *New Yorker*, May 5, 2008.

22 *And according to Classics scholars*: Marco Romani Mistretta, "Invention and Discovery in Greek and Roman Thought" (doctoral dissertation, Harvard University, Graduate School of Arts & Sciences, 2018).

23 *when people create, Simonton argues*: Dean Keith Simonton, *Origins of Genius: Darwinian Perspectives on Creativity* (New York: Oxford University Press, 1999).

25 *It's no coincidence that*: Karol Borowiecki, "The Origins of Creativity: The Case of the Arts in the United States Since 1850," *Discussion Papers on Business and Economics*, University of Southern Denmark, 3 (2019).

25 *In a clever series of experiments*: Melanie S. Brucks, "The Creativity Paradox: Soliciting Creative Ideas Undermines Ideation" (doctoral dissertation, Stanford University, 2019).

26 *Harvard professor Teresa Amabile*: Teresa M. Amabile, *Creativity in Context: Update to the Social Psychology of Creativity* (New York: Routledge, 2018).

26 *exposure to new images*: Morten Friis-Olivarius, Oliver J. Hulme, Martin Skov, Thomas Z. Ramsøy, and Hartwig R. Siebner, "Imaging the Creative Unconscious: Reflexive Neural Responses to Objects in the Visual and Parahippocampal Region Predicts State and Trait Creativity," *Scientific Reports* 7, no. 1 (2017): 14420.

26 *people from different cultures*: Angela Ka-yee Leung, William W. Maddux, Adam D. Galinsky, and Chi-yue Chiu, "Multicultural Experience Enhances Creativity: The When and How," *American Psychologist* 63, no. 3 (2008): 169.

26 *taking a walk outside*: Marily Oppezzo and Daniel L. Schwartz, "Give Your Ideas Some Legs: The Positive Effect of Walking on Creative Thinking," *Journal of Experimental Psychology: Learning, Memory, and Cognition* 40, no. 4 (2014): 1142.

26 *neuroimaging studies have found*: Andreas Fink, Karl Koschutnig, Mathias Benedek, Gernot Reishofer, Anja Ischebeck, Elisabeth M. Weiss, and Franz Ebner, "Stimulating Creativity via the Exposure to Other People's Ideas," *Human Brain Mapping* 33, no. 11 (2012): 2603–2610.

26 *Atwood draws extensively*: Margaret Atwood on the real-life events that inspired *The Handmaid's Tale* and *The Testaments*, September 9, 2019, https://www.penguin.co.uk /articles/2019/09/margaret-atwood-handmaids-tale-testaments-real-life-inspiration.

27 *"That's what's in the song"*: Joe Rogan, "Episode #1881: Rick Rubin," *Joe Rogan Experience*, October 12, 2022.

30 *Inspired by psychologist*: A. Aron, E. Melinat, E. N. Aron, R. D. Vallone, and R. J. Bator, "The Experimental Generation of Interpersonal Closeness: A Procedure and Some Preliminary Findings," *Personality and Social Psychology Bulletin* 23(4) (1997): 363–377.

Chapter 2. Originality Ostriches

35 *"There is something"*: Geraldine DeRuiter, "Bros., Lecce: We Eat at the Worst Michelin Starred Restaurant, Ever," December 6, 2021, *The Everywhereist*, https://www .everywhereist.com/2021/12/bros-restaurant-lecce-we-eat-at-the-worst-michelin -starred-restaurant-ever/.

38 *In fact, the biggest "hits"*: Brian Uzzi, Satyam Mukherjee, Michael Stringer, and Ben Jones, "Atypical Combinations and Scientific Impact," *Science* 342, no. 6157 (2013): 468–472.

39 *"It's like hip-hop"*: Doreen St. Félix, "Virgil Abloh, Menswear's Biggest Star: How the Creative Director Brought Something New to High Fashion," *New Yorker*, March 11, 2019.

39 *"Writers first searched"*: Raphael Falco, "How Bob Dylan Used the Ancient Practice of 'Imitatio' to Craft Some of the Most Original Songs of His Time," *The Conversation*, October 17, 2022.

43 *first US solo exhibition*: Nicholas Fox Weber, *Mondrian: His Life, His Art, His Quest for the Absolute* (New York: Alfred A. Knopf, 2024).

44 *In his grid paintings*: David Andrzejewski, David G. Stork, Xiaojin Zhu, and Ron Spronk, "Inferring Compositional Style in the Neo-plastic Paintings of Piet Mondrian by Machine Learning," Proceedings SPIE 7531, *Computer Vision and Image Analysis of Art* (February 16, 2010): 138–148, https://doi.org/10.1117/12.840558.

44 *"Anna was not like"*: Leo Tolstoy, *Anna Karenina* (Amazon, Kindle ed., 2023), 112–113.

45 *"She is a friend"*: Toni Morrison, *Beloved* (New York: Vintage, 2004), 331.

45 *"Free from the burden"*: Austin Kleon, *Steal Like an Artist: 10 Things Nobody Told You About Being Creative* (New York: Workman Publishing, 2012), 33.

46 *The researchers presented toddlers*: Derek E. Lyons, Andrew G. Young, and Frank C. Keil, "The Hidden Structure of Overimitation," *Proceedings of the National Academy of Sciences* 104, no. 50 (2007): 19751–19756.

47 *These films often took*: Jinhee Choi, *The South Korean Film Renaissance: Local Hitmakers, Global Provocateurs* (Middletown: Wesleyan University Press, 2011).

Chapter 3. Bottoms Up!

53 *In 2012, a retired*: Rob Williams, "How Much Is That Ferret in the Window? Argentinians Fall Victim to Scam as Pet Sellers Pass Off Fluffed-up Ferrets as Pedigree Poodles," *Independent*, April 8, 2013.

55 *"I did what"*: Howard Green, "Joanna Griffiths, CEO of Knix Intimate Apparel, Shares the Trials and Tribulations of Building a Business That Half the Population Can't Get Their Head Around," *Toronto Star*, March 17, 2022.

55 *"And I mean"*: Howard Green, "Joanna Griffiths," *Toronto Star*.

57 *They recruited thirty-one visual artists*: Jacob W. Getzels and Mihaly Csikszentmihalyi, *The Creative Vision: A Longitudinal Study of Problem Finding in Art* (New York: John Wiley & Sons, 1976).

59 *Instead, it was*: Jacob W. Getzels and Mihaly Csikszentmihalyi, "From Problem Solving to Problem Finding," in Irving Taylor, ed., *Perspectives in Creativity* (New York: Routledge, 2017), 90–116.

64 *"My writing felt like"*: Alice W. Flaherty, *The Midnight Disease: The Drive to Write, Writer's Block, and the Creative Brain* (New York: Houghton Mifflin Harcourt, 2004).

65 *temporal lobe epilepsy*: Kay R. Jamison, Robert H. Gerner, Constance Hammen, and Christine Padesky, "Clouds and Silver Linings: Positive Experiences Associated with Primary Affective Disorders," *American Journal of Psychiatry* 137, no. 2 (1980): 198–202.

65 *As Flaherty put it*: Scott Meyers, "*The Midnight Disease: The Drive to Write, Writer's Block and the Creative Brain*," Medium, "Go Into the Story," May 16, 2010, https://gointothestory.blcklst.com/the-midnight-disease-the-drive-to-write-writers-block-and-the-creative-brain-e560b1833ca6.

69 Significant Objects: Joshua Glenn and Rob Walker, eds., *Significant Objects* (Seattle, WA: Fantagraphics Books, 2012).

Part II. Gridding

73 *"In music, I've done tons"*: Emma Ingrissi, "On the Importance of Creative Agency," *The Creative Independent*, May 1, 2024, 3.

75 *the results of an impressive experiment*: Arnaldo I. Camuffo, Alfonso Gambardella, Danilo Messinese, Elena Novelli, Emilio Paolucci, and Chiara Spina, "A Scientific Approach to Entrepreneurial Decision-Making: Large-Scale Replication and Extension," *Strategic Management Journal* 45, vol. 6 (2024): 1209–1237.

Chapter 4. The Guiding Question

77 *"We had this artist"*: Susan K. Freedman, Danny Meyer, Erwin Wurm, and Joe DiStefano, "Food for Thought—and Art," *Public Art Works*, season 1, episode 2 (2020).

77 *"among the most"*: Frank Bruni, "A Daring Rise to the Top," *New York Times*, August 11, 2009.

78 *Even the name*: Randy Garutti and Mark Rosati, *Shake Shack: Recipes & Stories* (New York: Little, Brown, 2017).

80 *"Mr. Meyer runs"*: Pete Wells, "The Burger Remains a Work in Progress," *New York Times*, February 21, 2012.

80 *It was frozen*: Naveena Vijayan, "The Untold Truth of Shake Shack's Fries," *Mashed*, January 31, 2023.

83 *In Adam Moss's*: Adam Moss, *The Work of Art: How Something Comes from Nothing* (New York: Penguin, 2024).

84 *"It really just"*: Moss, *The Work of Art*, 75.

85 *Marie Van Brittan Brown had a specific*: Laura Hilgers, "A Brief History of the Home Security Alarm," *Smithsonian*, March 2021.

Chapter 5. Think Inside the Box

95 *Matisse sought to "discover"*: Henri Matisse, *Notes of a Painter*, https://www.arthistoryproject.com/artists/henri-matisse/notes-of-a-painter/ (1908).

95 *For the next forty years*: Magdalena Dabrowski, "Henri Matisse (1869–1954)," in *Heilbrunn Timeline of Art History*, Metropolitan Museum of Art (October 2004).

97 *It actually comes from*: Sam Loyd, *Sam Loyd's Cyclopedia of 5000 Puzzles Tricks and Conundrums with Answers* (The Lamb Publishing Company, 1914).

97 *In the 1970s*: Drew Boyd and Jacob Goldenberg, *Inside the Box* (London: Profile Books Ltd., 2013).

98 *"Overnight, it seemed"*: Drew Boyd, "Thinking Outside the Box: A Misguided Idea," *Psychology Today*, February 6, 2014.

99 *received the most constraints*: C. Page Moreau and Darren W. Dahl, "Designing the Solution: The Impact of Constraints on Consumers' Creativity," *Journal of Consumer Research* 32, no. 1 (2005): 13–22.

100 *research shows that*: Oguz A. Acar, Murat Tarakci, and Daan Van Knippenberg, "Creativity and Innovation Under Constraints: A Cross-disciplinary Integrative Review," *Journal of Management* 45, no. 1 (2019): 96–121.

100 *When Steven Spielberg*: Seth Jacobson, "When 'Jaws' Was Filming in MA Years Ago, the Set Was Plagued by Disaster. Here's a List," *Cape Cod Times*, July 6, 2024.

106 *In 1942, the Eameses*: Alexandra Griffith Winton, "Charles Eames (1907–78) and Ray Eames (1912–88)," in *Heilbrunn Timeline of Art History*, Metropolitan Museum of Art (August 2007).

107 *"When I'm writing well"*: Merve Emre, "Jon Dosse's Search for Peace," *New Yorker*, November 13, 2022.

107 *"There is something wonderful"*: George Saunders, "What Writers Really Do When They Write," *Guardian*, March 4, 2017.

107 *"Other characters are"*: Cheryl A. Ossola, "Sometimes the Story Writes Itself," *Writer's Digest*, June 10, 2019.

108 *Their research demonstrated*: Deena Skolnick and Paul Bloom, "The Intuitive Cosmology of Fictional Worlds," in Shaun Nichols, ed., *The Architecture of the Imagination: New Essays on Pretence, Possibility, and Fiction* (New York: Oxford University Press, 2006), 73.

108 *A related idea*: David Lewis, "Truth in Fiction," *American Philosophical Quarterly* 15, no. 1 (1978): 37–46.

109 *When we, as an author, imagine fictional*: Deena Skolnick Weisberg, "The Development of Imaginative Cognition," *Royal Institute of Philosophy Supplements* 75 (2014): 85–103.

Chapter 6. Transplanting

115 *The one catch?*: Mary Pilon, "Monopoly's Inventor: The Progressive Who Didn't Pass 'Go'," *New York Times*, February 13, 2015.

117 *"I often feel not so much"*: Tim Klein, interview with the author, March 26, 2025.

119 *Transplanting begins*: Keith J. Holyoak and Paul Thagard, *Mental Leaps: Analogy in Creative Thought* (Cambridge, MA: MIT Press, 1996).

119 *The solution came from*: Henry Tobias Jones, "Nakatsu's Kingfisher; or How Biomimicry Beat the Boom," Medium, January 21, 2018, https://medium.com/bells-whistles/gooddesign-baddesign-nakatsus-kingfisher-or-how-biomimicry-beat-the-boom-a91287d2d831.

119 *It also reduced*: Tom McKeag, "How One Engineer's Birdwatching Made Japan's Bullet Train Better," Trellis, October 19, 2012, https://trellis.net/article/how-one-engineers-birdwatching-made-japans-bullet-train-better/.

120 *One day, on a visit*: "Janet Stephens, Intrepid Hairdressing Archaeologist," *The History Blog*, January 12, 2012, http://www.thehistoryblog.com/archives/14729.

120 *Her discovery provided*: Janet Stephens, "Ancient Roman Hairdressing: On (Hair) Pins and Needles," *Journal of Roman Archaeology* 21 (2008): 110–132.

121 *"the engine of cognition"*: D. Gentner and L. Smith, "Analogical Reasoning," in V. S. Ramachandran, ed., *Encyclopedia of Human Behavior* (2d ed.) (Oxford, UK: Elsevier, 2012), 130–136.

121 *"Suppose you are"*: Mary L. Gick and Keith J. Holyoak, "Analogical Problem Solving," *Cognitive Psychology* 12, no. 3 (1980): 306–355.

123 *Fonstad's creative journey*: Brian Kevin, "Overlooked No More: Karen Wynn Fonstad, Who Mapped Tolkien's Middle Earth," *New York Times*, January 13, 2025.

124 *The French couple began skating*: Tatjana Flade, "France's Papadakis and Cizeron Reach for the Stars," *Golden Skate*, January 13, 2015.

125 *Ronald Burt, a pioneer*: Ronald S. Burt, *Brokerage and Closure: An Introduction to Social Capital* (New York: Oxford University Press, 2005).

126 *Libby's undergraduate research assistant*: Keith David Baich, *American Scientists, Americanist Archaeology: The Committee on Radioactive Carbon 14* (Portland: Portland State University, 2010).

127 *researchers at Indiana University*: Qing Ke, Emilio Ferrara, Filippo Radicchi, and Alessandro Flammini, "Defining and Identifying Sleeping Beauties in Science," *Proceedings of the National Academy of Sciences* 112, no. 24 (2015): 7426–7431.

Part III: Digging

133 *"It's like being a safe breaker"*: Elizabeth Murray, *Art 21*, "Humor," season 2, October 1, 2003.

Chapter 7. More Is More

137 *The most successful artists*: Dean Keith Simonton, "Thomas Edison's Creative Career: The Multilayered Trajectory of Trials, Errors, Failures, and Triumphs," *Psychology of Aesthetics, Creativity, and the Arts* 9 (2015): 2–14.

138 *"The best way"*: Jeremy Utley, "Have Lots of Ideas," Medium, September 15, 2021, https://medium.com/stanford-d-school/have-lots-of-ideas-3afc88f812a6.

138 *In a fascinating series*: Brian J. Lucas and Loran F. Nordgren, "The Creative Cliff Illusion," *Proceedings of the National Academy of Sciences* 117, no. 33 (2020): 19830–19836.

142 *In 1968, Spencer Silver*: Richard Sandomir, "Spencer Silver, an Inventor of Post-it Notes, Is Dead at 80," *New York Times*, May 13, 2021.

144 *The answer*: Samsun Knight, Matthew D. Rocklage, and Yakov Bart, "Narrative Reversals and Story Success," *Science Advances* 10, no. 34 (2024), https://www.science.org/doi/pdf/10.1126/sciadv.adl2013.

146 *a 2004 study*: Klaus K. Urban, "Assessing Creativity: The Test for Creative Thinking-Drawing Production (TCT-DP) the Concept, Application, Evaluation, and International Studies," *Psychology Science* 46, no. 3 (2004): 387–397.

147 *Other, more verbal tests*: Yoshiko Shimonaka and Katsuharu Nakazato, "Creativity and Factors Affecting Creative Ability in Adulthood and Old Age," *Japanese Journal of Educational Psychology* 55, no. 2 (2007): 231–243, https://doi.org/10.5926/jjep1953.55.2_231.

147 *And other research finds*: Anna N. N. Hui, Mavis W. J. He, and Wan-chi Wong, "Understanding the Development of Creativity Across the Life Span," in James C. Kaufman and Robert J. Sternberg, eds., *The Cambridge Handbook of Creativity* (Cambridge, UK: Cambridge University Press, 2019), 69–87.

147 *Among the directors*: Lu Liu, Yang Wang, Roberta Sinatra, C. Lee Giles, Chaoming Song, and Dashun Wang, "Hot Streaks in Artistic, Cultural, and Scientific Careers," *Nature* 559, no. 7714 (2018): 396–399.

Chapter 8. Search Far and Wide

156 *research suggests that when individuals*: Matthew P. Walker, Conor Liston, J. Allan Hobson, and Robert Stickgold, "Cognitive Flexibility Across the Sleep–Wake Cycle: REM-Sleep Enhancement of Anagram Problem Solving," *Cognitive Brain Research* 14, no. 3 (2002): 317–324.

156 *"I think also maybe"*: Branson Stousy, "Björk on Creativity as an Ongoing Experiment," *The Creative Independent*, December 14, 2017.

157 *To answer the question*: Justin M. Berg, "One-Hit Wonders versus Hit Makers: Sustaining Success in Creative Industries," *Administrative Science Quarterly* 67, no. 3 (2022): 630–673.

158 *When you compare Nobel*: Arne Güllich, Brooke N. Macnamara, and David Z. Hambrick, "What Makes a Champion? Early Multidisciplinary Practice, Not Early Specialization, Predicts World-Class Performance," *Perspectives on Psychological Science* 17, no. 1 (2022): 6–29.

159 *Sociologists Yonghoon Lee*: Yonghoon G. Lee and Martin Gargiulo, "Escaping the Survival Trap: Network Transition Among Early-Career Freelance Songwriters," *Administrative Science Quarterly* 67, no. 2 (2022): 339–377.

160 *the "strength of weak ties"*: Mark S. Granovetter, "The Strength of Weak Ties," *American Journal of Sociology* 78, no. 6 (1973): 1360–1380.

161 *large-scale analysis*: Agata Fronczak, Maciej J. Mrowinski, and Piotr Fronczak, "Scientific Success from the Perspective of the Strength of Weak Ties," *Scientific Reports* 12, no. 1 (2022): 5074.

161 *when managers at a large company*: Markus Baer, "The Strength-of-Weak-Ties Perspective on Creativity: A Comprehensive Examination and Extension," *Journal of Applied Psychology* 95, no. 3 (2010): 592.

161 *in times of business distress*: Daniel M. Romero, Brian Uzzi, and Jon Kleinberg, "Social Networks Under Stress," in *Proceedings of the 25th International Conference on World Wide Web* (2016), 9–20.

167 *In 2022, Melanie Brucks*: Melanie S. Brucks and Jonathan Levav, "Virtual Communication Curbs Creative Idea Generation," *Nature* 605, no. 7908 (2022): 108–112.

Chapter 9. The Spark

172 *One striking insight from these sketches*: Robert W. Weisberg, "On Structure in the Creative Process: A Quantitative Case-Study of the Creation of Picasso's *Guernica*," *Empirical Studies of the Arts* 22, no. 1 (2004): 23–54.

172 *"[Picasso's] thought did not range"*: Weisberg, "On Structure in the Creative Process."

173 *"No chef ever"*: Jerry Paffendorf, "Staying True to the Idea: No Chef Ever Takes Credit for Making the Fish," *The Regrid Blog*, October 18, 2023.

174 *"She speaks earnestly"*: Stephen King, *On Writing: A Memoir of the Craft* (New York: Scribner, 2000), 165.

175 *Consumer researchers*: Laura J. Kornish and Karl T. Ulrich, "The Importance of the Raw Idea in Innovation: Testing the Sow's Ear Hypothesis," *Journal of Marketing Research* 51, no. 1 (2014): 14–26.

178 *Consider InnoVAE*: Zhaoqi Cheng, Dokyun Lee, and Prasanna Tambe, "InnoVAE: Generative AI for Mapping Patents and Firm Innovation" (March 1, 2022), available at SSRN 3868599.

180 *Led by Dokyun Lee*: Eric Zhou and Dokyun Lee, "Generative Artificial Intelligence, Human Creativity, and Art," *PNAS Nexus* 3, no. 3 (2024): 052.

181 *write a short story*: Anil R. Doshi and Oliver P. Hauser, "Generative AI Enhances Individual Creativity but Reduces the Collective Diversity of Novel Content," *Science Advances* 10, no. 28 (2024): eadn5290.

181 *In the end*: Shakked Noy and Whitney Zhang, "Experimental Evidence on the Productivity Effects of Generative Artificial Intelligence," *Science* 381, no. 6654 (2023): 187–192.

182 *In the hands of someone*: Ethan Mollick, *Co-Intelligence* (London: W. H. Allen, 2024).

182 *"Creativity consists of both"*: Dokyun Lee, interview with the author, March 8, 2025.

Part IV: Sifting

189 *"Stories are relics"*: King, *On Writing*, 163–164.

Chapter 10. Create by Subtracting

194 *"My typical style"*: Stephen Holden, "Paul Simon Brings Home the Music of Black South Africa," *New York Times*, August 24, 1986.

195 *People often fail to see*: Gabrielle S. Adams, Benjamin A. Converse, Andrew H. Hales, and Leidy E. Klotz, "People Systematically Overlook Subtractive Changes," *Nature* 592, no. 7853 (2021): 258–261.

194 *but frequently overlooked strategy*: Leidy Klotz, *Subtract: The Untapped Science of Less* (New York: Flatiron Books, 2021).

198 *filmmaker and comedian Taika Waititi*: Julia Camara, "How Taika Waititi Writes a Script: 5 Screenwriting Tips," *We Screenplay Blog*, October 29, 2020, https://www.wescreen play.com/blog/taika-waititi-screenwriting-tips/.

202 *"You can sometimes"*: *Mike Birbiglia's Working It Out*, episode 155, "David Sedaris Returns: A Creative's Dream and a Fact-checker's Nightmare," December 30, 2024.

204 *"[Y]ou can fail"*: Jim Carrey, commencement speech, Maharishi University of Management, May 30, 2014, rev.com, https://www.rev.com/transcripts/jim-carrey-commencement -speech-transcript-2014-at-maharishi-university-of-management.

Chapter 11. How Ideas *Feel*

211 *Ed Sheeran*: Jon Pareles, "How Ed Sheeran Made 'Shape of You' the Year's Biggest Track," *New York Times*, December 20, 2017.

213 *"If we were to describe"*: Max Wertheimer, *Productive Thinking* (New York: Harper & Row, 1959).

215 *behavioral economist George Loewenstein*: George Loewenstein, "The Psychology of Curiosity: A Review and Reinterpretation," *Psychological Bulletin* 116, no. 1 (1994): 75.

215 *organizational psychologist Justin Berg*: Justin M. Berg, "When Silver Is Gold: Forecasting the Potential Creativity of Initial Ideas," *Organizational Behavior and Human Decision Processes* 154 (2019): 96–117.

216 *"Here's what happened"*: Moss, *The Work of Art*, 25.

216 *Of this, Moss writes*: Moss, *The Work of Art*, 22.

217 *research by psychologists*: John Angus D. Hildreth and Cameron Anderson, "Failure at the Top: How Power Undermines Collaborative Performance," *Journal of Personality and Social Psychology* 110, no. 2 (2016): 261.

218 *In one elegant demonstration*: Claudia M. Mueller, and Carol S. Dweck, "Praise for Intelligence Can Undermine Children's Motivation and Performance," *Journal of Personality and Social Psychology* 75, no. 1 (1998): 33.

218 *"If you're thought a genius"*: Quote Investigator, May 17, 2010.

218 *When economist*: Fabian Bocart, Marina Gertsberg, and Rachel A. J. Pownall, "An Empirical Analysis of Price Differences for Male and Female Artists in the Global Art Market," *Journal of Cultural Economics* 46, no. 3 (2022): 543–565.

219 *a 2023 meta-analysis*: Christa L. Taylor, Sameh Said-Metwaly, Anaëlle Camarda, and Baptiste Barbot, "Gender Differences and Variability in Creative Ability: A Systematic Review and Meta-analysis of the Greater Male Variability Hypothesis in Creativity," *Journal of Personality and Social Psychology* 126, no. 6 (June 2024): 1161–1179.

219 *research by Laura Tian*: Laura Tian, "Implicit Gender Inferences Diminish Evaluations of Female Artists' Work" (PhD dissertation, University of Toronto, 2022).

219 *contexts, such as business proposals*: Devon Proudfoot, Aaron C. Kay, and Christy Z. Koval, "A Gender Bias in the Attribution of Creativity: Archival and Experimental Evidence for the Perceived Association Between Masculinity and Creative Thinking," *Psychological Science* 26, no. 11 (2015): 1751–1761.

220 *We found that instead*: Andrea C. Vial, Melis Muradoglu, George E. Newman, and Andrei Cimpian, "An Emphasis on Brilliance Fosters Masculinity-Contest Cultures," *Psychological Science* 33, no. 4 (2022): 595–612.

Chapter 12. The Learning Curve

227 *For every doubling*: Theodore P. Wright, "Factors Affecting the Cost of Airplanes," *Journal of the Aeronautical Sciences* 3, no. 4 (1936): 122–128.

227 *For example, a research paper*: Yian Yin, Yang Wang, James A. Evans, and Dashun Wang, "Quantifying the Dynamics of Failure Across Science, Startups and Security," *Nature* 575, no. 7781 (2019): 190–194.

229 *"Many of life's failures"*: Deborah Headstrom-Page, *From Telegraph to Light Bulb with Thomas Edison* (Nashville, TN: B&H Publishing, 2007).

230 *"You're digging away"*: Ed Catmull and Amy Wallace, *Creativity, Inc. (The Expanded Edition): Overcoming the Unseen Forces That Stand in the Way of True Inspiration* (New York: Random House, 2014).

230 *mega pop star Dua Lipa*: Jack Irvin, "Dua Lipa Reveals She 'Wrote 97 Songs' in a 'Random Notebook' from CVS for Her Upcoming Album," *People*, February 9, 2024.

230 *Jordan Peele revealed*: *Conan O'Brien Needs a Friend Podcast*, Jordan Peele, Monday, January 1, 2024.

Conclusion: Getting Unstuck

248 *Take the unexpected case*: Kate Bernot, "How a New Pasta Shape Changed the Way I Think About Cooking," *America's Test Kitchen*, April 13, 2021.

Appendix: Deeper Questions About Creativity

251 *Even a beaver's dam*: Richard Dawkins, *The Extended Phenotype* (Oxford: Oxford University Press, 1982).

252 *"Thus, nature gets credit"*: Alfred North Whitehead, *Science and the Modern World* (London: Cambridge University Press, 1932).

257 *even today scientists*: Jodi D.G. Kooijman, Jaap P. Meijaard, Jim M. Papadopoulos, Andy Ruina, and Arend L. Schwab, "A Bicycle Can Be Self-Stable Without Gyroscopic or Caster Effects," *Science* 332, no. 6027 (2011): 339–342.

258 *At the age of fifteen*: R. Lacasse, *Joseph-Armand Bombardier: An Inventor's Dream Come True* (Montreal: Canada Libre Expression, 1988).

258 *known as the* adjacent possible: Stuart A. Kauffman, *Investigations* (New York: Oxford University Press, 2000).

258 *and later popularized*: Steven Johnson, *Where Good Ideas Come From: The Natural History of Innovation* (New York: Penguin, 2011).

259 *Carl Eliason in Wisconsin patented*: Wisconsin Historical Society, Carl Eliason 1899–1979.

259 *Virgil White from New Hampshire*: Marguerite Andrews, "The Machine in the Forest: A Political Ecology of Snowmobiling and Conflict in Maine's North Woods" (PhD dissertation, Rutgers University-Graduate School-New Brunswick, 2008).

Index